SHAKESPEARE

A MIDSUMMER NIGHT'S DREAM

COLES EDITORIAL BOARD

Bound to stay open

Publisher's Note

Otabind (Ota-bind). This book has been bound
using the patented Otabind process You can
open this book at any page, gently run your
finger down the spine, and the pages will lie flat

ABOUT COLES NOTES

COLES NOTES have been an indispensible aid to students on five continents since 1948.

COLES NOTES are available for a wide range of individual literary works. Clear, concise explanations and insights are provided along with interesting interpretations and evaluations.

Proper use of COLES NOTES will allow the student to pay greater attention to lectures and spend less time taking notes. This will result in a broader understanding of the work being studied and will free the student for increased participation in discussions.

COLES NOTES are an invaluable aid for review and exam preparation as well as an invitation to explore different interpretive paths.

COLES NOTES are written by experts in their fields. It should be noted that any literary judgement expressed herein is just that – the judgement of one school of thought. Interpretations that diverge from, or totally disagree with any criticism may be equally valid.

COLES NOTES are designed to supplement the text and are not intended as a substitute for reading the text itself. Use of the NOTES will serve not only to clarify the work being studied, but should enhance the readers enjoyment of the topic.

ISBN 0-7740-3217-0

© COPYRIGHT 2003 AND PUBLISHED BY
COLES PUBLISHING COMPANY
TORONTO - CANADA
PRINTED IN CANADA

Manufactured by Webcom Limited
Cover finish: Webcom's Exclusive **DURACOAT**

CONTENTS

Page No.

WILLIAM SHAKESPEARE: LIFE AND WORKS

Biographical Sketch 1
Shakespeare's Writings 3
Shakespeare's England 6
The Elizabethan Theater 9
Shakespeare's Artistry 11

A MIDSUMMER NIGHT'S DREAM

Introduction 15
Description of The Play 17
The Title of The Play 19
Characterisation 20
Plot Summary 21

Critical Analysis Of The Play

ACT I	• SCENE 1	23
	SCENE 2	29
ACT II	• SCENE 1	33
	SCENE 2	41
ACT III	• SCENE 1	45
	SCENE 2	51
ACT IV	• SCENE 1	59
	SCENE 2	64
ACT V	• SCENE 1	65

Character Sketches

Theseus 69
Hippolyta 70
Hermia 70
Helena 71
Lysander 72
Demetrius 72
Egeus 72
Bottom 73
Peter Quince, Francis Flute,
Tom Snout, Robin Starveling 73
Oberon 74
Titania 74
Puck 75
Peaseblossom, Cobweb, Moth, Mustardseed 75
Philostrate 75

Theme 75

Points of Interest 76

A Contrast Between
A Midsummer Night's Dream and *The Tempest* .. 80

A Midsummer Night's Dream:
Critical Appraisal 80

Shadow and Substance in
A Midsummer Night's Dream 86

The Element of Imagination In
A Midsummer Night's Dream 91

The Supernatural In
A Midsummer Night's Dream 97

Selected Criticisms 108

Review Questions and Answers 112

Bibliography 122

WILLIAM SHAKESPEARE
LIFE AND WORKS

Biographical Sketch

With the epithet "Dear Son of Memory", Milton praised Shakespeare as one constantly in our memories and brother of the Muses. Certainly no other author has held such sway over the literary world, undiminished through some three and a half centuries of shifting artistic tastes. Shakespeare's plots and his characters have continued to be a living reality for us; as his well known contemporary Ben Jonson wrote, in a familiar tribute, "Thou . . . art alive still, while thy Booke doth live,/ And we have wits to read, and praise to give."

The Early Years

Despite such acclaim and the scholarship it has spawned, our knowledge of Shakespeare's life is sketchy, filled with more questions than answers, even after we prune away the misinformation accumulated over the years. He was baptized on April 26, 1564, in Holy Trinity Church, Stratford-on-Avon. As it was customary to baptize children a few days after birth, we conjecture that he was born on April 23. The monument erected in Stratford states that he died on April 23, 1616, in his fifty-third year.

William was the third child of John Shakespeare, who came to Stratford from Snitterfield before 1532 as a "whyttawer" (tanner) and glover, and Mary Arden, daughter of a wealthy "gentleman of worship" from Wilmecote. They married around 1557. Since John Shakespeare owned one house on Greenhill Street and two on Henley Street, we cannot be certain where William was born, though the Henley Street shrine draws many tourists each year. William's two older sisters died in infancy, but three brothers and two other sisters survived at least into childhood.

Shakespeare's father was fairly well-to-do, dealing in farm products and wool, and owning considerable property in Stratford. After holding a series of minor municipal offices he was elected alderman in 1565, high bailiff (roughly similar to the mayor of today) in 1568, and chief alderman in 1571. There are no records of young Will Shakespeare's education (though there are many unfounded legends), but he undoubtedly attended the town school maintained by the burgesses, which prepared its students for the universities. Ben Jonson's line about Shakespeare's having "small *Latine*, and lesse *Greeke*" refers not to his education but to his lack of indebtedness to the classical writers and dramatists.

On November 27, 1582, a licence to marry was issued to "Willelmum Shaxpere *et* Annam Whateley *de* Temple Grafton," and on

1

the next day a marriage bond for "Willm Shagspere" and "Anne Hathwey of Stratford" was signed by Fulk Sandells and John Richardson, farmers of Stratford. This bond stated that there was no "lawful let or impediment by reason of any precontract, consanguinity, affinity, or by any other lawful means whatsoever"; thus "William and Anne (were) to be married together with once asking of the banns of matrimony." The problem of Anne Whateley has led many researchers and some detractors to argue all kinds of improbabilities, such as the existence of two different Shakespeares and the forging of documents to conceal Shakespeare's true identity. The actual explanation seems to be simple: the clerk who made the marriage licence entry apparently copied the name "Whateley" from a preceding entry, as a glance at the full sheet suggests. (Incidentally, Nicholas Rowe in his life of Shakespeare, published in 1709, well before the discovery of these marriage records, gave Anne's name as Hathaway.) The problems of marriage with Anne Hathaway — he was eighteen and she was twenty-six — and of the bond have caused similar consternation. Why did these two marry when there was such a discrepancy of age? Why only one saying of the banns (rather than the usual three)? Why the emphasis on a possible legal impediment? The answer here is not simple or definite, but the birth of a daughter Susanna, baptized at Holy Trinity on May 26, 1583, seems to explain the odd circumstances. It should be recognized, however, that an engagement to marry was considered legally binding in those days (we still have breach-of-promise suits today) and that premarital relations were not unusual or frowned upon when an engagement had taken place. The circumstances already mentioned, Shakespeare's ensuing activities, and his will bequeathing to Anne "my second best bed with the furniture" have suggested to some that their marriage was not entirely happy. Their other children, the twins Hamnet and Judith, were christened on February 2, 1585.

Theatrical Life

Shakespeare's years before and immediately after the time of his marriage are not charted, but rumor has him as an apprentice to a master butcher or as a country teacher or an actor with some provincial company. He is supposed to have run away from whatever he was doing for livelihood and to have gone to London, where he soon attached himself to some theatrical group. At this time there were only two professional houses established in the London environs, The Theatre (opened in 1576) and The Curtain (opened in 1577). His first connection with the theater was reputedly as holder of horses; that is, one of the stage crew, but a most inferior assignment. Thereafter he became an actor (perhaps at this time he met Ben Jonson), a writer, and a director. Such experience had its mark in the theatricality of his plays. We do know that he was established in London by 1592, when Robert Greene

2

lamented in *A Groatsworth of Wit* (September, 1592) that professional actors had gained priority in the theater over university-trained writers like himself: "There is an upstart Crow, beautified with our feathers, that with his *Tygers hart wrapt in a Players hyde*, supposes he is as well able to bombast out a lanke verse as the best of you: and beeing an absolute *Iohannes fac totum* (Jack-of-all-trades), is in his owne conceit the onely Shake-scene in a countrey." An apology for Greene's ill-humored statement by Henry Chettle, the editor of the pamphlet, appeared around December 1592 in *Kind-Hart's Dream*.

Family Affairs

To return to the known details of family life, Shakespeare's son Hamnet was buried at Stratford on August 11, 1596; his father was given a coat of arms on October 20, 1596; and he purchased New Place (a refurbished tourist attraction today) on May 4, 1597. The London playwright obviously had not severed connections with his birthplace, and he was reflecting his new affluence by being known as William Shakespeare of Stratford-upon-Avon, in the County of Warwick, Gentleman. His father was buried in Stratford on September 8, 1601; his mother, on September 9, 1608. His daughter Susanna married Dr. John Hall on June 5, 1607, and they had a child named Elizabeth. His other daughter, Judith, married Thomas Quiney on February 10, 1616, without special licence, during Lent and was thus excommunicated. Shakespeare revised his will on March 25, 1616, and was buried on April 25, 1616 (according to the parish register). A monument by Gerard Janssen was erected in the Holy Trinity chancel in 1623 but many, like Milton several years later, protested:

> What needs my *Shakespeare* for his honour'd Bones,
> The labour of an age in piled Stone, . . .
> Thou in our wonder and astonishment
> Hast built thy self a live-long Monument.

Shakespeare's Writings

Order of Appearance

Dating of Shakespeare's early plays, while based on inconclusive evidence, has tended to hover around the early 1590's. Almost certainly it is his chronicles of Henry the Sixth that Philip Henslowe, an important theatrical manager of the day, referred to in his diary as being performed during March-May 1592. An allusion to these plays also occurs in Thomas Nashe's *Piers Penniless His Supplication to the Devil* (August, 1592). Greene's quotation about a tiger is a paraphrase of "O tiger's heart wrapt in a woman's hide" from *Henry VI*, Part III.

The first published work to come from Shakespeare's hand was *Venus and Adonis* (1593), a long stanzaic poem, dedicated to Henry

Wriothesley, Earl of Southampton. A year later *The Rape of Lucrece* appeared, also dedicated to Southampton. Perhaps poetry was pursued during these years because the London theaters were closed as a result of a virulent siege of plague. The *Sonnets*, published in 1609, may owe something to Southampton, who had become Shakespeare's patron. Perhaps some were written as early as the first few years of the 1590's. They were mentioned (along with a number of plays) in 1598 by Francis Meres in his *Palladis Tamia*, and sonnets 138 and 144 were printed without authority by William Jaggard in *The Passionate Pilgrim* (1599).

There is a record of a performance of *A Comedy of Errors* at Gray's Inn (one of the law colleges) on December 28, 1594, and, during early 1595, Shakespeare was paid, along with the famous actors Richard Burbage and William Kempe, for performances before the Queen by the Lord Chamberlain's Men, a theatrical company formed the year before. The company founded the Globe Theatre on the south side of the Thames in 1599 and became the King's Men when James ascended the throne. Records show frequent payments to the company through its general manager John Heminge. From 1595 through 1614 there are numerous references to real estate transactions and other legal matters, to many performances, and to various publications connected with Shakespeare.

Order of Publication

The first plays to be printed were *Titus Andronicus* around February, 1594, and the garbled versions of *Henry VI*, Parts II and III in 1594. (Some scholars, however, question whether the last two are versions of *Henry VI*, Parts II and III, and some dispute Shakespeare's authorship.) Thereafter *Richard III* appeared in 1597 and 1598; *Richard II*, in 1597 and twice in 1598; *Romeo and Juliet*, in 1597 (a pirated edition) and 1599, and many others. Some of the plays appear in individual editions, with or without Shakespeare's name on the title page, but eighteen are known only from their appearance in the first collected volume (the so-called First Folio) of 1623. The editors were Heminge and Henry Condell, another member of Shakespeare's company. *Pericles* was omitted from the First Folio although it had appeared in 1609, 1611, and 1619; it was added to the Third Folio in 1664.

There was reluctance to publish plays at this time for various reasons; many plays were carelessly written for fast production; collaboration was frequent; plays were not really considered *reading* matter; they were sometimes circulated in manuscript; and the theatrical company, not the author, owned the rights. Those plays given individual publication appeared in a quarto, so named from the size of the page. A single sheet of paper was folded twice to make four leaves (thus *quarto*) or eight pages; these four leaves constitute one signature (one section of a bound book). A page measures about 6¾ in. x 8½ in. On the other hand, a folio sheet is folded once to make two leaves or four pages; three sheets, or twelve pages, constitute a signature. The page is approximately 8½ in. x 13⅜ in.

Authorized publication occurred when a company disbanded, when money was needed but rights were to be retained, when a play failed or ran into licensing difficulties (thus, hopefully, the printed work would justify the play against the criticism), or when a play had been pirated. Authorized editions are called good quartos. Piratical publication might occur when the manuscript of a play had circulated privately, when a member of a company desired money for himself, or when a stenographer or memorizer took the play down in the theater (such a version was recognizable by inclusion of stage directions derived from an eyewitness, by garbled sections, etc.). Pirated editions are called bad quartos; there are at least five bad quartos of Shakespeare's plays.

Authenticity of Works

Usually thirty-seven plays are printed in modern collections of Shakespeare's works but some recent scholars have urged the addition of two more: *Edward III* and *Two Noble Kinsmen*. A case has also been advanced, unconvincingly, for a fragment of the play on Sir Thomas More. At times, six of the generally-accepted plays have been questioned: *Henry VI*, Parts I, II and III, *Timon of Athens*, *Pericles* and *Henry VIII*. The first four are usually accepted today (one hopes all question concerning *Timon* has finally ended), but if Shakespeare did not write these plays in their entirety, he certainly wrote parts of them. Of course, collaboration in those days was commonplace. Aside from the two long narrative poems already mentioned and the sonnets (Nos. 1-152, but not Nos. 153-154), Shakespeare's poetic output is uncertain. *The Passionate Pilgrim* (1599) contains only five authenticated poems (two sonnets and three verses from *Love's Labour's Lost*); *The Phoenix and the Turtle* (1601) may be his, but the authenticity of *A Lover's Complaint* (appended to the sonnets) is highly questionable.

Who Was Shakespeare?

At this point we might mention a problem that has plagued Shakespeare study for over a century: who was Shakespeare? Those who would like to make the author of the plays someone else — Francis Bacon or the Earl of Oxford or even Christopher Marlowe (dead long before most of the plays were written) — have used the lack of information of Shakespeare's early years and the confusion in the evidence we have been examining to advance their candidate. But the major arguments against Shakespeare show the source of these speculators' disbelief to be in classconscious snobbery and perhaps in a perverse adherence to minority opinion. The most common argument is that no one of Shakespeare's background, lack of education, and lack of aristocratic experience could know all that the author knew. But study will reveal that such information was readily available in various popular sources, that some of it lies in the literary sources used for the play, and that Shakespeare was probably not totally lacking in education or in social decorum. The more significant question of style and tone is not dealt with — nor could it successfully be raised. Bacon, for example, no matter how much we admire his mind and his writings, exhibits a writing style diametrically opposite to Shakespeare's, a style most unpoetic and often flat. The student would be wise not to waste time rehashing these unfounded theories. No such question was raised in the seventeenth or eighteenth centuries, and no serious student of the plays today doubts that Shakespeare *was* Shakespeare.

Shakespeare's Plays

Exact dates for Shakespeare's plays remain a source of debate among scholars. The following serve only as a general frame of reference.

	COMEDIES	TRAGEDIES	HISTORIES
1591			Henry VI, Part I
1592	Comedy of Errors		Henry VI, Part II
1592	Two Gentlemen of Verona		Henry VI, Part III
1593	Love's Labour's Lost	Titus Andronicus	Richard III
1594			King John
1595	Midsummer Night's Dream	Romeo and Juliet	Richard II
1596	Merchant of Venice		
1596	Taming of the Shrew		
1597			Henry IV, Part I
1598	Much Ado About Nothing		Henry IV, Part II
1599	As You Like It	Julius Caesar	
1599	Merry Wives of Windsor		Henry V
1601	Twelfth Night	Hamlet	
1602	Troilus and Cressida		
1602	All's Well That Ends Well		
1604	Measure for Measure	Othello	
1605		King Lear	
1606		Macbeth	
1607		Timon of Athens	
1607		Antony and Cleopatra	
1608	Pericles		
1609		Coriolanus	
1610	Cymbeline		
1611	Winter's Tale		
1611	Tempest		
1613			Henry VIII

Shakespeare's England

The world of Elizabethan and Jacobean England was a world of growth and change. The great increase in the middle class, and in the population as a whole, demanded a new economy and means of livelihood, a new instrument of government (one recognizing "rights" and changed class structure), a new social code and a broad base of entertainment. The invention of printing a century before had contributed to that broader base, but it was the theater that supplied the more immediate needs of the greatest numbers. The theater grew and along with it came less-educated, more money-conscious writers, who gave the people what they wanted: entertainment. But Shakespeare, having passed through a brief period of hack writing, proceeded to set down important ideas in memorable language throughout most of his career. His plays, particularly the later ones, have been analyzed by recent critics in terms of literary quality through their metaphor, verse-line, relationships with psychology and myth, and elaborate structure. Yet Shakespeare was a man of the stage, and the plays were written to be performed. Only this will fully account for the humor of a deadly serious play like *Hamlet* or the spectacle of a *Coriolanus*.

Life in London

During Shakespeare's early years there, London was a walled city of about 200,000, with seven gates providing access to the city from the east, north, and west. It was geographically small and crisscrossed by narrow little streets and lanes. The various wards each had a parish church that dominated the life of the close-knit community. To the south and outside were slums and the haunts of criminal types, and farther out were the agricultural lands and huge estates. As the population increased and the central area declined, the fashionable people of the city moved toward the west, where the palace of Westminster lay. Houses were generally rented out floor by floor and sometimes room by room. Slums were common within the city, too, though close to pleasant enough streets and squares. "Merrie Olde England" was not really clean, nor were its people, for in those days there were no sewers or drains except the gutter in the middle of the street, into which garbage would be emptied to be floated off by the rain to Fleet ditch or Moor ditch. Plague was particularly ravaging in 1592, 1593-94 (when the theaters were closed to avoid contamination) and 1603. Medical knowledge, of course, was slight; ills were "cured" by amputation, leeching, blood-letting and cathartics. The city was (and still is) dominated by St. Paul's Cathedral, around which booksellers clustered on Paternoster Row.

Religious Atmosphere

Of great significance for the times was religion. Under Elizabeth, a state church had developed; it was Protestant in nature and was called Anglican (or today, Episcopalian) but it had arisen from Henry VIII's break with the Pope and from a compromise with the Roman Catholics who had gained power under Mary Tudor.

The Church of England was headed by the Archbishop of Canterbury, who was to be an increasingly important figure in the early part of the seventeenth century. There were also many schismatic groups, which generally desired further departures from Roman Catholicism. Calvinists were perhaps the most numerous and important of the Protestant groups. The Puritans, who were Calvinist, desired to "purify" the church of ritual and certain dogmas, but during the 1590's they were lampooned as extremists in dress and conduct.

Political Milieu

During Shakespeare's lifetime there were two monarchs: Elizabeth, 1558-1603, and James I, 1603-1625. Elizabeth was the daughter of Henry VIII and Anne Boleyn, his second wife, who was executed in 1536. After Henry's death, his son by his third wife, Jane Seymore (died in 1537), reigned as Edward VI. He was followed by Mary Tudor, daughter of Henry's first wife, Catherine of Aragon. Mary was a Roman Catholic, who tried to put down religious dissension by persecution of both Protestants and Catholics. Nor did her marriage to Philip II of Spain endear her to the people.

Elizabeth's reign was troubled by many offers of marriage, particularly from Spanish and French nobles — all Roman Catholic — and by the people's concern for an heir to the throne. English suitors generally cancelled one another out by intrigue or aggressiveness. One of the most prominent was the Earl of Essex, Robert Devereux, who fell in and out of favor; he apparently attempted to take over the reins of control, only to be captured, imprisoned and executed in February, 1601. One claimant to the throne was Mary of Scotland, a Roman Catholic and widow of Francis II of France. She was the second cousin of Elizabeth, tracing her claim through her grandmother, who was Henry VIII's sister. Finally, settlement came with Elizabeth's acceptance of Mary's son as heir apparent, though Mary was to be captured, tried and executed for treason in 1587. Mary had abdicated the throne of Scotland in 1567 in favor of her son, James VI. His ascent to the throne of England in 1603 as James I joined the two kingdoms for the first time, although Scotland during the seventeenth century often acted independently of England.

Contemporary Events

Political and religious problems were intermingled in the celebrated Gunpowder Plot. Angry over fines that were levied upon those not attending Church of England services — primarily Roman Catholics — and offended by difficulties over papal envoys, a group of Catholics plotted to blow up Parliament, and James with it, at its first session on November 5, 1605. A cache of gunpowder was stored in the cellar, guarded by various conspirators, among them Guy Fawkes. The plot was discovered before it could be carried out and Fawkes, on duty at the time, was apprehended. The execution of the plotters and the triumph of the anti-Papists led in succeeding years to celebrations in the streets and the hanging of Fawkes in effigy.

Among the most noteworthy public events during these times were the wars with the Spanish, which included the defeat of the Spanish Armada in 1588, the battle in the Lowlands in 1590-1594, the expedition to Cadiz under Essex in 1596 and the expedition to the Azores (the Islands Expedition), also under Essex, in 1597. With trading companies especially set up for colonization and exploitation, travel excited the imagination of the people: here was a new way of life, here were new customs brought back by the sailors and merchants, here was a new dream world to explore.

In all, the years from around 1590 to 1601 were trying ones for English people, relieved only by the news from abroad, the new affluence and the hope for the future under James. Writers of the period frequently reflect, however, the disillusionment and sadness of those difficult times.

The Elizabethan Theater

Appearance

The Elizabethan playhouse developed from the medieval inn with its rooms grouped around a courtyard into which a stage was built. This pattern was used in The Theatre, built by James Burbage in 1576: a square frame building (later round or octagonal) with a square yard, three tiers of galleries, each jutting out over the one below, and a stage extending into the middle of the yard, where people stood or sat on improvised seats. There was no cover over the yard or stage and lighting was therefore natural. Thus performances were what we might consider late matinees or early evening performances; in summer, daylight continues in London until around ten o'clock.

Other theaters were constructed during the ensuing years: The Curtain in 1577, The Rose in 1587 (on Bankside), The Swan in 1595 (also Bankside) and Shakespeare's playhouse, The Globe, in 1599 (not far from The Rose). There is still some question about the exact dimensions of this house, but it seems to have been octagonal, each side measuring about 36 feet, with an over-all diameter of 84 feet. It was about 33 feet to the eaves, and the yard was 56 feet in diameter. Three sides were used for backstage and to serve the needs of the players. There was no curtain or proscenium, hence the spectators became part of the action. Obviously, the actors' asides and soliloquies were effective under these conditions.

There was no real scenery and there were only a few major props; thus the lines of the play had to reveal locations and movement, changes in time or place, etc. In this way, too, it was easier to establish a nonrealistic setting, for all settings were created in words. On either side of the stage were doors, within the flooring were trapdoors (for entrances of ghosts, etc.), and behind the main stage was the inner stage or recess. Here, indoor scenes (such as a court or a bedchamber) were played, and some props could be used because the inner stage was usually concealed by a curtain when not in use. It might also have served to hide someone behind the ever-present arras, like Polonius in *Hamlet*. The "chamber" was on the second level, with windows and a balcony. On the third level was another chamber, primarily for musicians.

Actors

An acting company such as the Lord Chamberlain's Men was a fellowship of ten to fifteen sharers with some ten to twelve extras, three or four boys (often to play women's roles) who might become full sharers, and stagehands. There were rival companies, each with its leading dramatist and leading tragic actor and clown. The Lord Admiral's Men, organized in 1594, boasted Ben Jonson and the tragedian Edward Alleyn. Some of the rivalry of this War of the Theaters is reflected in the speeches of Hamlet, who also comments on the ascendancy and unwarranted popularity of the children's companies (like the Children of Blackfriars) in the late 1590's.

The company dramatist, of course, had to think in terms of the members of his company as he wrote his play. He had to make use of the physical features and peculiar talents of the actors, making sure, besides, that there was a role for each member. The fact that women's parts were taken by boys imposed obvious limitations on the range of action. Accordingly, we often find women characters impersonating men; for example, Robert Goffe played Portia in *The Merchant of Venice*, and Portia impersonates a male lawyer in the important trial scene. Goffe also played Juliet, and Anne in *Richard III*, and Oberon in *Midsummer-Night's Dream*. The influence of an actor on the playwright can be seen, on the one hand, by noting the "humor" characters portrayed so competently by Thomas Pope, who was a choleric Mercutio in *Romeo*, a melancholic Jaques in *As You Like It*, and a sanguinary Falstaff in *Henry IV*, Part I; and by comparing, on the other hand, the clown Bottom in *Midsummer-Night's Dream*, played in a frolicsome manner by William Kempe, with the clown Feste in *Twelfth Night*, sung and danced by Robert Armin. Obviously, too, if a certain kind of character was not available within the company, then that kind of character could not be written into the play. The approach was decidedly different from ours today, where the play almost always comes first and the casting of roles second. The plays were performed in a repertory system, with a different play each afternoon. The average life of a play was about ten performances.

History of the Drama

English drama goes back to native forms developed from playlets presented at Church holidays. Mystery plays dealt with biblical stories such as the Nativity or the Passion, and miracle plays usually depicted the lives of saints. The merchant and craft guilds that came to own and produce the cycles of plays were the forerunners of the theatrical companies of Shakespeare's time. The kind of production these cycles received, either as moving pageants in the streets or as staged shows in a churchyard, influenced the late sixteenth-century production of a secular play: there was an intimacy with the audience and there was a great reliance on words rather than setting and props. Similar involvement with the stage action is experienced by audiences of the arena theatre of today.

The morality play, the next form to develop, was an allegory of the spiritual conflict between good and evil in the soul of man. The *dramatis personae* were abstract virtues and vices, with at least one man representing Mankind (or Everyman, as the most popular of these plays was titled). Some modern critics see *Othello* as a kind of morality play in which the soul of Othello is vied for by the aggressively evil Iago (as a kind of Satanic figure) and passively good Desdemona (as a personification of Christian faith in all men). The Tudor interlude — a short, witty, visual play — may have influenced the subplot of the Elizabethan play with its low-life and jesting and visual tricks. In mid-sixteenth century appeared the earliest known English comedies, Nicholas Udall's *Ralph Roister Doister* and *Gammer Gurton's Needle* (of uncertain authorship). Both show the influence of the Roman comic playwright Plautus. Shakespeare's *Comedy of Errors*, performed in the 1590's, was an adaptation of Plautus' *Menaechmi*, both plays featuring twins and an involved story of confused identities. The influence of the Roman tragedian Seneca can be traced from Thomas Norton and Thomas Sackville in *Gorboduc* to *Hamlet*. Senecan tragedy is a tragedy of revenge, characterized by many deaths, much blood-letting, ghosts, feigned madness and the motif of a death for a death.

Shakespeare's Artistry

Plots

Generally, a Shakespearean play has two plots: a main plot and a subplot. The subplot reflects the main plot and is often concerned with inferior characters. Two contrasting examples will suffice: Lear and his daughters furnish the characters for the main plot of filial love and ingratitude, whereas Gloucester and his sons enact the same theme in the subplot; Lear and Gloucester both learn that outward signs of love may be false. In *Midsummer-Night's Dream*, the town workmen (Quince, Bottom *et al.*) put on a tragic play in such a hilarious way that it turns the subject of the play — love so strong that the hero will kill himself if his loved one dies first — into farce, but this in the main plot is the "serious" plight of the four mixed-up lovers. In both examples Shakespeare has reinforced his points by subplots dealing with the same subject as the main plot.

11

Sources

The plots of the Elizabethan plays were usually adapted from other sources. "Originality" was not the sought quality; a kind of variation on a theme was. It was felt that one could better evaluate the playwright's worth by seeing what he did with a familiar tale. What he stressed, how he stressed it, how he restructured the familiar elements — these were the important matters. Shakespeare closely followed Sir Thomas North's very popular translation of Plutarch's *Life of Marcus Antonius*, for example, in writing *Antony and Cleopatra*; and he modified Robert Greene's *Pandosto* and combined it with the Pygmalion myth in *The Winter's Tale*, while drawing the character of Autolycus from certain pamphlets written by Greene. The only plays for which sources have not been clearly determined are *Love's Labour's Lost* (probably based on contemporary events) and *The Tempest* (possibly based on some shipwreck account from travelers to the New World).

Verse and Prose

There is a mixture of verse and prose in the plays, partially because plays fully in verse were out of fashion. Greater variety could thus be achieved and character or atmosphere could be more precisely delineated. Elevated passages, philosophically significant ideas, speeches by men of high rank are in verse, but comic and light parts, speeches including dialect or broken English, and scenes that move more rapidly or simply give mundane information are in prose. The poetry is almost always blank verse (iambic pentameter lines without rhyme). Rhyme is used, however (particularly the couplet), to mark the close of scenes or an important action. Rhyme also serves as a cue for the entrance of another actor or some off-stage business, to point to a change of mood or thought, as a forceful opening after a passage of prose, to convey excitement or passion or sentimentality and to distinguish characters.

Shakespeare's plays may be divided into three general categories, though some plays are not readily classified and further subdivisions may be suggested within a category.

The History Play

The history play, or chronicle, may tend to tragedy, like *Richard II*, or to comedy, like *Henry IV*, Part I. It is a chronicle of some royal personage, often altered for dramatic purposes, even to the point of falsification of the facts. Its popularity may have resulted from the rising of nationalism of the English, nurtured by their successes against the Spanish, their developing trade and colonization, and their rising prestige as a world power. The chronicle was considered a political guide, like the popular *Mirror for Magistrates*, a collection of writings showing what happens when an important leader falls through some error in his ways, his thinking or his personality. Thus the history play counseled the right path by negative, if not positive, means. Accordingly, it is difficult to call *Richard II* a tragedy, since Richard was wrong and his wrongness harmed his people. The political philosophy of Shakespeare's day seemed to favor the view that all usurpation was bad and should be corrected, but not by further usurpation. When that original usurpation had been established, through an heir's ascension to the throne, it was to be accepted. Then any rebellion against the "true" king would be a rebellion against God.

Tragedy

Tragedy in simple terms meant that the protagonist died. Certain concepts drawn from Aristotle's *Poetics* require a tragic hero of high standing, who must oppose some conflicting force, either external or internal. The tragic hero should be dominated by a *hamartia* (a so-called tragic flaw, but really an *excess* of some character trait, e.g., pride, or *hubris*), and it is this *hamartia* that leads to his downfall and, because of his status, to the downfall of others. The action presented in the tragedy must be recognizable to the audience as real and potential: through seeing it enacted, the audience has its passion (primarily suffering) raised, and the conclusion of the action thus brings release from that passion (*catharsis*). A more meaningful way of looking at tragedy in the Elizabethan theater, however, is to see it as that which occurs when essential good (like Hamlet) is wasted (through disaster or death) in the process of driving out evil (such as Claudius represents).

Comedy

Comedy in simple terms meant that the play ended happily for the protagonists. Sometimes the comedy depends on exaggerations of man's eccentricities — comedy of humors; sometimes the comedy is romantic and far-fetched. The romantic comedy was usually based on a mix-up in events or confused identity of characters, particularly by disguise. It moved toward tragedy in that an important person might die and the mix-up might never be unraveled; but in the nick of time something happens or someone appears (sometimes illogically or unexpectedly) and saves the day. It reflects the structure of myth by moving from happiness to despair to resurrection. *The Winter's Tale* is a perfect example of this, for the happiness of the first part is banished with Hermione's exile and Perdita's abandonment; tragedy is near when the lost baby, Perdita, cannot be found and Hermione is presumed dead, but Perdita reappears, as does Hermione, a statue that suddenly comes to life. Lost identities are established and confusions disappear but the mythic-comic nature of the play is seen in the reuniting of the mother, Hermione, a kind of Ceres, with her daughter, Perdita, a kind of Prosperina. Spring returns, summer will bring the harvest, and the winter of the tale is left behind — for a little while.

What is it, then, that makes Shakespeare's art so great? Perhaps we see in it a whole spectrum of humanity, treated impersonally, but with kindness and understanding. We seldom meet in Shakespeare a weeping philosopher: he may criticize, but he criticizes both sides. After he has done so, he gives the impression of saying, Well, that's the way life is; people will always be like that — don't get upset about it. This is probably the key to the Duke's behavior in *Measure for Measure* — a most unbitter comedy despite former labels. Only in *Hamlet* does Shakespeare not seem to fit this statement; it is the one play that Shakespeare, the person, enters.

As we grow older and our range of experience widens, so, too, does Shakespeare's range seem to expand. Perhaps this lies in the ambiguities of his own materials, which allow for numerous individual readings. We meet our own experiences — and they are ours alone, we think — expressed in phrases that we thought our own or of our own discovery. What makes Shakespeare's art so great, then, is his ability to say so much to so many people in such memorable language: he is himself "the show and gaze o' the time."

A MIDSUMMER NIGHT'S DREAM
Introduction

A Midsummer Night's Dream is the best of Shakespeare's early comedies. It is, in fact, the best comedy written in English before 1597. None of his plays is more exuberant or more joyful. An idealistic fancy in which rustics, lovers, fairies and royalty alternately hold sway, it anticipates his last play, *The Tempest,* both in its original plot and in its reliance on fairy magic. But it is more light-hearted, more playful – the fantasy of a younger man.

There has been some question as to the date and the occasion of the play's first performance. The first printed edition, the First Quarto of 1600, stated that it had been "sundry times publicly acted." Earlier, in 1598, Francis Meres in his *Palladis Tamia: Wits Treasury* mentioned it as one of the comedies responsible for Shakespeare's fame. Given the opening speeches and the closing epithalamium, few critics have doubted that it was originally written for an important wedding. On such occasions the Elizabethan nobility expected spectacular entertainment. Interludes, masques, pageants, with elaborate costumes and scenic devices, formed the order of the day. Most critics believe that the play was written to honor the marriage of William Stanley, Earl of Derby, whose father and brother had been patrons of Shakespeare's acting company, to Elizabeth Vere, daughter of the Earl of Oxford, on January 26, 1595. However, A. L. Rowse, in his *William Shakespeare* (Harper & Row, 1963), declares that the play was first performed the night before the wedding of the Countess of Southampton and Sir Thomas Heneage, which took place on May 2, 1594. Shakespeare gathered up into one festive comedy the different kinds of pageantry that were usually presented piecemeal at such an event. The resulting mixture was so skilfully blended that, as one critic has remarked, it is hard not to feel that this play alone is worth all of his other romances.

As the play was occasioned by a marriage, so within the play itself the marriage of Theseus and Hippolyta provides the frame. As the play celebrates the happy culmination of a love, so its action centers around the plight of four lovers and brings about their happiness. The fairies, essential mythology in the celebration of nuptials, here become controlling characters in the action. And the play itself presents an entertainment for the wedding party, as does the rustics' production of *Pyramus and Thisbe* within the play.

As the joyful celebration provides a key to an understanding of the play's unity, so too it provides, in part, a key to the sources. *A Midsummer Night's Dream* is one of the few Shakespearean dramas for which no trace of the plot as a whole has been found in any earlier play or story. The sources are to be found in the various forms of popular entertainment, in the folklore associated with marriages, in the pageants and the masques that the Elizabethans knew very well. They are to be found, too, in the literature available to the age. The legend of Theseus appears in Chaucer's *Knight's Tale* as well as in Plutarch's *Lives* (translated by Thomas North in 1579) and Ovid's *Metamorphoses.*

Oberon, king of the Faery, can be found in the French romance of Huon of Bordeaux which had been translated into English about 1540, and in Spenser's *The Faerie Queene*. The name Titania is used as an epithet of Diana and of Circe the enchantress in Ovid's *Metamorphoses*. Bottom's transformation recalls that in Apuleius' *Golden Ass*, translated by Richard Aldington in 1566. The Pyramus and Thisbe story also appears in the *Metamorphoses*.

But the play that Shakespeare produced is more than an excellent 16th-century entertainment for the Court. As he took some of his folklore from books, so he transformed his court revel into an uniquely Elizabethan form of comedy – one he had used before in *Two Gentlemen from Verona* and one he was to use again and again. Romantic comedy, a genre unique to Elizabethan England, had as its origin the prose romance which was very popular in the 16th century. Painter's *Palace of Pleasure*, Greene's *Pandosto*, Lodge's *Rosalinde*, and Sidney's *Arcadia* were earlier prototypes of Greene's play, *Friar Bacon and Friar Bungay*, the first of the romantic comedies, soon followed by Peele's *Old Wives' Tale*. And these, in turn, as much as the court masques, were the forerunners of *A Midsummer Night's Dream*.

In its transference to the stage, romantic comedy retained characteristics usually associated with narrative fiction. Its effects derive from the handling of atmosphere and romantic accident rather than from psychological interpretation of character or dramatic intrigue. It depends on imaginary atmosphere, half pastoral, half fairy, and upon a series of absorbing adventures which befall the characters and for which they are rarely responsible. It is notable for the absence of fundamental dramatic conflict and for the absence of practical logic from the drive of characters and emotions. It is just such a story of love and sylvan adventure, of fairies and lovers in a magic wood, that Shakespeare tells in *A Midsummer Night's Dream*.

Greene depended for the success of his comedies upon the inclusion of a great variety of possible sources of interest. Shakespeare too plays with multiple worlds and multiple plots. There are four different groups of characters presented: the rulers, the lovers, the rustics, and the fairies; if one includes Pyramus and Thisbe, there are five different stories. We are presented with fancy, realism, courtliness, bawdy, sentiment, and poetry. Few plays have as much richness and variety of incident, character, diction and verse. But in the wood of Athens the divided worlds meet and mingle. With the consummate skill of the young but accomplished dramatist Shakespeare, out of this variety of incident and character evolved a single theme.

It is at Theseus' wedding that Hermia's fate is to be decided. It is to celebrate this wedding that the fairies have come from India. It is for this wedding that Bottom and his fellows are practicing. It is Bottom with whom Titania falls in love. It is because of Oberon that Demetrius returns to his first love, Helena. All together watch the presentation of *Pyramus and Thisbe* at the end. And the fairies exorcise and bless the wedding chambers.

The triumphant manner in which the poet reduces to harmony the incongruities, anachronisms, contradictions, and impossible juxtapositions of *A Midsummer Night's Dream*, in itself would make this play a masterpiece.

The play is, as Shakespeare reminds us, a midsummer night's dream. The action occurs mostly at night, characters are forever falling asleep and dreaming, and the movement itself is dependent on the whims of fairies. Sometimes a bush may seem to be a bear, but, conversely, a bloody lion is revealed as no more than a rustic's disguise; and the whole substance of the play is a shadow. It is, like *Romeo and Juliet,* a play about love in which "young bright things come to confusion." But it is love as interpreted by the comic rather than the tragic spirit – a certain fine lunacy in the brain of youth, an enchantment of fairies. As Bottom remarks, "reason and love keep little company together nowadays." Love's Maytime sprouting is an ecstasy; its forever-after happiness is a midsummer night's dream.

Description of the Play

A Midsummer Night's Dream is a sort of ideal dream, and stands in a class by itself. It most resembles a masque but as we shall see it differs from a masque in several important respects. In spite of its irregularities we should note some of its leading characteristics.

Harmonious Blending of Different Elements

The play comprises four different histories: that of Theseus and Hippolyta, of the four Athenian lovers, of the 'home-spun' actors, and of the fairies. Shakespeare has invented the fairy machinery by means of which he has been able to blend together the apparently incongruous elements, the courtiers and the clowns. The complication of the plot, or plots, all or nearly all the actions of the characters, and the unravelling of the entanglements do not in *A Midsummer Night's Dream,* as they do in Shakespeare's other plays, proceed from the inner impulse of the actors, but all come from without. The fairies serve as motive forces for nearly all the other actors. Taking the place of the classical god Cupid, they form the link of connection.

Use of the Lyrical Element

Lyric poetry is poetry originally intended to be accompanied by the lyre or by some other musical instrument. The term has come to signify any outburst in song which is composed under a strong impulse of emotion or inspiration. Shakespeare has not only given to *A Midsummer Night's Dream* a lyrical character, by interspersing songs here and there in the play, but, as Coleridge has said, 'the whole of *A Midsummer Night's Dream* is one continual specimen of the dramatised lyrical.'

Dream-Like Character

We shall deal with this more fully when we come to discuss the title of the play. For now it is sufficient to point out that the play resembles a dream in its wonderful complications, its lawlessness, its ideality, and its disregard of the laws of time and place.

Resemblance to a Masque

In *A Midsummer Night's Dream* the masque 'imperceptibly glides into comedy', but it still retains many of the distinctive features of the more showy form of entertainment. It resembles a masque in the following points:

1.   In its general lyrical character, and in the special introduction of music and dances.

2.   In the fact that in this play the delineation of character is a secondary object.

3.   In its adaptability for out-of-door representation.

4.   In the predominance of classical and mythical names.

5.   In the use of the farcical interlude or anti-masque. The love-stories of Theseus and the Athenian youths form a kind of framework into which the anti-masque is inserted, the fairies corresponding to some extent with the choruses of dances of the regular masque.

6.   In the fact that the play has all the appearance of having been originally intended, like the masques, for private entertainment, probably to celebrate the marriage of some noble.

Difference from a Masque

1.   In that it is much longer than ordinary masques.

2.   It is more dramatic and full of human interest.

3.   It contains blank verse, unlike traditional masques.

4.   It exhibits little of the profound classical learning found in those produced by Ben Jonson. Shakespeare has popularized the subject and borrowed freely from both classical and medieval fables.

Humor

The comic element of the play is, of course, to be found principally in those scenes in which Bottom and his fellow craftsmen display their happy imbecility, and these scenes are in themselves so irresistibly comic, that we can hardly feel surprise when we read that 'The merry conceited humours of Bottom the Weaver', were, at the period of the Restoration converted into a farce, and acted apart from the rest of the play. The incongruity between what the actors really are, and what they pretend to be, is the very essence of what is laughable: and Bottom's absolute unconsciousness of what others think of him, very much heightens the absurdity of the situation. But it is a mistake to think that by separating these comic scenes from their framework that you are extracting the best part of the humor of the play. Shakespeare was rarely content with what is merely comical; most often he carried his comedy to the verge of the serious, and mingled his mirth with beauty or pathos as in *A Midsummer Night's Dream*.

This is the way of real life. A noted critic, Dr. Dowden, reminds us that: "The traditions of the English drama had favoured the juxtaposition of the serious and comic; but it was reserved for Shakespeare to make each a part of the other; to interpenetrate tragedy with comedy, and comedy with tragic earnestness."

It is when the comic characters, Bottom and his *confrères* pass into the serious parts of the drama that they really infect it with the element of humor. Nothing, for example, could be more powerfully humorous than the scene in which Titania bids her fairies to minister to the desires of Bottom.

The Title of the Play

In considering the fitness of the title which Shakespeare has chosen for his fairy comedy, we naturally ask ourselves two questions, 'Why is it called a Dream?' and 'Why is the dream associated with Midsummer Night?'

The Play regarded as a Dream

Shakespeare has made it very evident by numerous passages in the play that he did not intend this comedy to be regarded from the same point of view as other plays, or to be judged by the laws that govern the drama of character and life. At the end of the play, in the lines which stand in the place and bear the character of an Epilogue, Puck asks his audience to think:

> That you have but slumber'd here
> While these visions did appear.
> And this weak and idle theme,
> No more yielding but a dream,
> Gentles do not reprehend.

> (Act V, Sc. 1, 428)

The actions of the principal characters during the greater part of the play are performed while under the influence of illusion and enchantment, so that the actors themselves are no more masters and mistresses of their own thoughts, words, and conduct than if they were actually

> Begot of nothing but vain fantasy
> Which is as thin of substance as the air
> And more inconstant than the wind
> (*Romeo and Juliet*, Act IV, Sc. 1)

Titania, on being released from the spell that had been laid upon her, exclaims: 'What visions have I seen!' (Act IV, Sc. 1, 77). Lysander, Hermia, Helena and Demetrius relate their dreams to the Duke and Duchess, and Theseus regards them as 'antique fables and fairy toys'. The delicate and airy verse, the beautiful and tender imagery, the shadowy characterisation and the atmosphere of fairy-land all fit in admirably with the idea of a dream.

Midsummer Night Associations

We have seen that the play is appropriately called a Dream and now enquire, "Why, when the action of the play belongs to the end of April and the first of May, should it be associated in the title with Midsummer Night" (June 24th or St. John the Baptist's Day)? Two reasons suggest themselves in answer to our question.

1. It may have been specially written for performance on that day.

2. There may be in the play something specially connected with, or recalling, the traditional observances of that day.

In view of our lack of definite knowledge as to the actual occasion (if any) for which the play was composed, and in the absence of definite information as to the date of the composition of the play we are unable to offer any argument in support of the first view except this: that judging from its masque-like character it appears to have been written for some particular occasion and that (as is doubtless the fact in the case of *Twelfth Night* and *A Winter's Tale*, a tale 'to beguile the dreary leisure of a long winter evening'), it may have derived its title from that occasion.

With respect to the second view we must take particular notice of two things (1) that many superstitious notions of a highly fanciful character were formally connected with St. John's Eve, and (2) that Shakespeare himself seems to allude to such superstitions in *Twelfth Night* when Olivia describes the strange behaviour of Malvolio as 'very midsummer madness'. Consequently, whatever may have been the circumstance that led Shakespeare to adopt his title for the play, we are justified in saying that the title chosen is a most appropriate one.

Characterisation

Shakespeare is distinguished from all his contemporaries (and from all subsequent dramatists) by his skill in depicting character. This excellence is not so apparent in *A Midsummer Night's Dream* as it is in his later plays, for, not only had he not yet developed his powers to their full extent, but he is limited by the nature of the play itself, its fantastical dream-like quality, in which the action is usually prompted from outside and does not so much proceed from the characters of the play as it does in his great tragedies and, to a less extent, in his later comedies.

Nevertheless, even in his early play Shakespeare has portrayed some unforgettable characters which are completely individual, while others, without being individualistic are always true to type. Sir John Squire has written, "Characters swarmed from Shakespeare's brain as (though mostly in the easier form of caricatures) they swarmed from Dickens's; and he had an unparalleled power, by virtue of imagination, genius and craftsman's cunning, of making them comprehensible and memorable in a few sentences, of giving the mind the significant bones from which the whole skeleton could be automatically deduced." (*Shakespeare as a Dramatist,* Cassell and Company)

For the student of Shakespeare's plays the following simple rules are useful in studying the nature of a character.

1. Take into account what is said of him (or her) by other characters in the play, at the same time having regard to the speaker whether he is friend or enemy or neutral.

2. Consider what the person says of himself, especially in soliloquy.

3. Watch him in action and draw conclusions.

4. Look out for contrasts. Characters in Shakespeare are often found in pairs and their contrast may be illuminating, e.g. Hermia and Helena.

5. Note carefully any descriptions of the appearance of the character.

6. Observe tricks of speech, remembering that Shakespeare's persons usually speak in character. The duke does not speak as does the carpenter, nor the fairy as the mortal. Everything that Bottom says contributes towards our knowledge of him.

7. Put yourself in the place of each character in the play, imagine his feelings, try to re-live his life, get to know him as you know (or think you know) yourself.

Plot Summary

The play opens in the palace of Theseus, Duke of Athens. Theseus is a mythical Greek hero. He is about to marry Hippolyta, Queen of the Amazons, a mythical race of women-warriors. Hermia's father, Egeus, comes before the Duke to ask that she be punished by law for disobeying him. Hermia wants to marry Lysander and Egeus wants her to marry Demetrius. The law he asks to be invoked provides that she die or enter a nunnery if she doesn't obey her father. We learn that Demetrius, her father's choice, has abandoned Helena. Helena still loves her unfaithful Demetrius. Lysander and Hermia plan to elope. They tell Helena, who says she'll tell Demetrius. All four lovers will go to the woods the next night: Hermia and Lysander to elope; Demetrius to prevent this, having been warned by Helena; and Helena herself to be with Demetrius. Thus, at this point a situation that was all right before the play began is now off balance, with the two men loving Hermia, and Helena sad and lovelorn.

In the next scene we are introduced to an entirely different group of characters. A number of Athenian workmen – Quince, Bottom, Flute, Snout, Snug, and Starveling – have come together to prepare a play as entertainment after the Duke's wedding. Their play is "Pyramus and Thisbe," a traditional tale of tragic love. Young lovers are separated by the animosity of their parents and through an error they kill themselves. These simple workmen are comically inept in their theatrical venture. One of their company, Bottom the weaver, is remarkable for his enthusiasm and self-confidence. He wants to play all the parts and gives examples of his ability. These characters agree to meet in the woods the next night to rehearse their play.

Next we enter another entirely different world. We are now in the wood mentioned in both of the previous scenes, and we meet Puck, or Robin Goodfellow, a mischievous spirit known for household pranks and rustic devilment. He is the helpmate of Oberon, King of the Fairies, whom we also meet here. We witness a quarrel between the King and his Queen, Titania. The Queen has a changeling that the King wants and she will not give him the boy. To get what he wants, Oberon plans to enchant the Queen's eyes with a love-juice that will cause her to fall madly in love with anyone or anything she sees. While she's thus diverted, he'll get the changeling. Oberon sends Puck to obtain the flower possessing this magic juice. The King witnesses Helena's one-sided love for Demetrius and when Puck returns he is instructed to apply the juice to Demetrius so that he'll love Helena.

The plot begins to thicken, for Puck anoints the eyelids of Lysander, who wakes and loves Helena. Helena has been deserted by Demetrius and when Lysander suddenly declares that he loves her she feels abused and leaves to continue looking for Demetrius. Lysander follows her, leaving Hermia asleep. Hermia wakes after he is gone and goes to look for him. The situation has been made worse, for now neither man loves the woman who loves him: Hermia loves Lysander, but Lysander loves Helena; Helena loves Demetrius, but Demetrius loves Hermia.

Titania has been enchanted by Oberon and awaits being awakened by her "beloved." Having seen our first group, the lovers, it is time to pick up our second group, the workmen. Therefore we now are with Bottom and his companions and they are rehearsing in the wood very near Titania's sleeping-place. Puck chances on the scene and he puts an ass's head on Bottom. The other workmen flee in fright and Bottom sings to show his courage, even though he's quite frightened himself, not knowing why they've run away. Titania is awakened by Bottom's song and she loves him, ass's head and all.

Hermia and Demetrius meet in the wood and by witnessing their conversation, Oberon sees that Puck has enchanted the wrong Athenian. In order to remedy the situation, he'll charm Demetrius. Now Helena and Lysander meets Demetrius, so events are at the height of confusion because *both* men claim to love Helena. This is the reverse of the beginning, when neither loved her. Hermia has been seeking Lysander. When she finds him, she finds also that he no longer loves her. All she can come up with in the way of an explanation is that Helena has stolen Lysander away by comparing her height to Hermia's small stature. Helena thinks the three others have banded together to make fun of her. The two girls quarrel. Finally Oberon has Puck apply a curative to Lysander so that he'll love Hermia again. Demetrius remains enchanted so that he'll love Helena.

Puck has told Oberon how Titania has fallen in love with the transformed Bottom. The King gets his changeling and then takes the charm off Titania. The lovers are awakened by Theseus, Hippolyta and Egeus. They can't say how it came about, but everything is finally right. The Duke declares that they'll have a triple wedding. Last to awaken is Bottom, who rightly declares the unfathomability of his "dream" and feels most profoundly its power. When he returns to his fellow workmen, we see their mutual affection and concern. We learn that their play of "Pyramus and Thisbe" is to be performed at court.

Finally, the wedding of Theseus and Hippolyta mentioned at the very beginning of the play takes place. Hermia and Lysander, Helena and Demetrius are married also. The workmen present their play amid much comment from the males present. After the household is asleep, the fairies enter and bless everything with peace and prosperity. Puck's last words to us suggest that the whole thing may be only a dream, and thus concludes *A Midsummer Night's Dream*.

Critical Analysis of the Play
ACT I · SCENE 1

The play opens in the palace of Theseus, Duke of Athens, a legendary Greek hero. He enters accompanied by his bride-to-be Hippolyta, queen of the Amazons. Theseus tells Hippolyta that although their wedding is only four days away, his impatience makes the time seem long. She answers that the interval will pass quickly. Both measure time by the moon – it is waning now and will be a new crescent on the night of their marriage. Theseus sends Philostrate, who is in charge of entertainment at the court, into the city to organize the public celebration of the wedding, and contrasts this planned merriment with his conquering Hippolyta initially in his war on the Amazons.

COMMENT: *The play's theme of love and marriage is announced strongly and immediately by the opening exchange of speeches between Theseus and Hippolyta (pronounced Hip-pól-i-ta). The repeated mention of the moon is important to note here, for it is mentioned often throughout the play. Shakespeare learned of Theseus from North's translation of Plutarch's* Lives of the Noble Grecians and Romans. *To Shakespeare and his contemporaries, Theseus was not legend but historical fact. Shakespeare also knew of Theseus from Chaucer's* Knight's Tale. *One of Theseus' legendary heroic exploits was his successful war on the Amazons, a mythical nation of women-warriors. Hippolyta's comment on how quickly time will pass is noteworthy because we shall see that indeed time does strange things when love is governing events.*

Egeus, father of Hermia, comes before the Duke to complain about his daughter. He explains that while Demetrius has his consent to marry her, she has been "bewitched" by Lysander and wants to marry him, thus being disobedient. Accordingly Egeus asks that the law be enforced which provides for either her obedience or her death. Theseus questions Hermia, advising her that her father's authority over her is absolute and likening the relationship between father and daughter to that between a mold and wax. In reply to Theseus' declaration that Demetrius is worthy, she says that Lysander is, too. Theseus says that her father's approval makes Demetrius worthier, where-upon she counters with the wish that her father saw with her eyes. Theseus replies that her eyes must rather be governed by her father's judgment. She asks what may happen to her if she refuses to wed Demetrius. The Duke replies that she must die or become a nun, "chanting faint hymns to the cold, fruitless moon."

She must consider well whether she can undergo a life which, unlike a "rose distilled," rather withers "on the virgin thorn" and "grows, lives and dies in single blessedness." Hermia avows she would rather do thus than marry Demetrius because her father commands it. Theseus says she should think it over and announce her decision on the night of his marriage to Hippolyta. Demetrius and Lysander now exchange sharp words and, in presenting his case, Lysander reveals that there is a further complication. Demetrius has been false to Helena, who is still in love with him even though he has forsaken her by switching his affection to Hermia. Theseus says he's heard of this and he leaves with Hippolyta, taking Demetrius and Egeus with him. Lysander and Hermia are thus left alone on the stage to comment on their situation and plan what to do about it.

COMMENT: *With the entrance of Egeus, the threads of the plot begin to emerge. The typical disgruntled father, he straight away announces this: "Full of vexation come I." His description of how Lysander has won Hermia away from proper obedience to her father's wishes is the classic view of the older, stolid generation toward young and wayward romance. Balconies by moonlight, love poetry, souvenirs, gifts of jewelry, flowers, and candy are all a silly nuisance. These interfere with the orderly, business-like fulfilment by a dutiful daughter of a marriage contract made by a responsible father. Thus, the play's treatment of the theme of love and marriage is given the added dimension of Egeus' unfavorable view of courtship here, and the harsh penalty he asks be imposed against the kind of romance he decries will serve to advance the plot when Hermia and Lysander try to escape this penalty. The use of one's eyes in love is introduced here. We shall see that how well one "sees" where love is concerned is a crucial question in the play, and that linking judgment to vision is not as easy as Theseus would imply. The description of the relationship between Egeus and Hermia as similar to that between a mold and wax was frequently applied in Shakespeare's time to the parent-child relationship, and also to the authority of men over women, whose minds were considered particularly impressionable and susceptible to the stronger male influence.*

Theseus' speech on "single blessedness" mentions the moon and uses a rose in its famous characterization of single and married life, both references being in keeping with the play's special mood and atmosphere. Shakespeare uses similarly the idea of a flower distilled into perfume in a sonnet where he is speaking of how men may perpetuate themselves by having children. Though both Lysander and Demetrius love Hermia now, we learn here that Demetrius loved another girl, Helena, previously, and that she still loves him. Hermia does not want Demetrius, but Helena does. No one wants Helena, while both men claim Hermia. They were once in love mutually and if Demetrius were still so, the other pair, whose love is mutual – Hermia and Lysander – would have no trouble.

Left alone, Hermia and Lysander discuss their situation, and Lysander remarks, ''the course of true love never did run smooth.'' He suggests that they solve their problem by eloping the next night. He will meet Hermia in the woods outside of town and take her to his aunt's house, which is seven leagues away. A league is usually estimated at roughly three miles nowadays. There, free of Athenian law, they may marry. Hermia agrees, swearing ''by all the vows that ever men have broke'' that she will keep the appointment.

COMMENT: *Although this thwarted love between Hermia and Lysander contains the ingredients of tragedy, we see here that the treatment is decidedly in a lighter, comic vein. Rather than a display of great passion and emotional strife, the foregoing speeches are so stylized and formal that what we observe are the typical young lovers in the typical thwarted romance. We are meant to respond to this and are kept from feeling the deeper, stronger, more tragic emotions which are potentially present. A league is a very indefinite measure, and combined with the fairy-tale number, seven, the distance becomes a story-book journey through the woods to auntie's house. The measurement of distance, like that of time pointed out earlier, is adjusted to suit the play's own world, a world at whose center is a dream. Two obvious examples of the stylized formality noted in the lovers' comments above are first, a type of dramatic dialogue called stichomythia, where characters speak single alternating lines (lines 136-140). It is worth noticing here because it is an extremely formal device, occurring very rarely in Shakespeare, but present again in this play and noted as such below. Secondly, the smoothness of the famous platitude about the course of true love not being smooth is a give-away to the emotional content here – it's a little too pat for a man really in the throes of deep suffering. It is interesting to note also that Hermia swears by the vows that men have broken. We shall see that in this play the men are inconstant in a comical degree.*

Helena, Demetrius's forsaken but still doting girlfriend, now comes upon the scene. When Hermia addresses her as ''fair Helena,'' her immediate reaction is to tell of her unhappy love for Demetrius. Helena says she herself is not fair since Demetrius loves Hermia's beauty. She wishes appearance were contagious the way sickness is so that she might be just like Hermia and so win back Demetrius.

COMMENT: *Hermia and Helena here speak in alternating single* *lines of dialogue (lines 194-201), another case of stichomythia as explained above and again achieving an extremely formal, stiff effect. The sing-song of the contrast between the way Demetrius treats each girl takes the bite out of Helena's sad situation, and prevents us from taking it seriously.*

To comfort Helena, Hermia and Lysander tell her about their plan to meet the next night in the woods by moonlight and elope. After they leave, Helena speaks her mind. She says love has transforming power. Cupid is a blind and wing'd boy because love does not see with the eyes but with the mind, does not involve the judgment, and is often perjured.

COMMENT: *In the theater of Shakespeare, a character often thinks out loud this way, and by this means, called a soliloquy, we in the audience know his mind. Helena's reference to transformation should be noted here. She also mentioned it when she wished she might catch Hermia's appearance like one does a sickness. Transformation is a very important theme in the play, and will be dealt with more fully as it reappears throughout. The relation of love to eyesight and vision is connected to the idea of transformation. We should note that Helena's mention of eyes and judgment here recalls the exchange on the subject noted earlier between Theseus and Hermia. Eyesight and judgment, vision and transformation are questions of first importance in this play. Helena's mentioning perjury in love echoes Hermia's swearing to meet Lysander, by all the vows that men have broken.*

Now Helena refers to Demetrius' inconstancy and resolves to tell him of the planned elopement, betraying her friend so that she may win Demetrius' gratitude and, more important, follow him to the woods and thereby have his company.

Notes

In this scene we learn the following:

1. Theseus and Hippolyta are to be married.

2. Hermia and Lysander want to be married, but

3. Egeus, Hermia's father, wants her to marry Demetrius.

4. Demetrius is loved by Helena, whom he loved before his present attachment to Hermia.

5. All four lovers will go to the woods the next night: Hermia and Lysander to elope; Demetrius to prevent this, having been warned by Helena; and Helena herself to be with Demetrius.

THESEUS   This mythical king or ruler of Athens, called a duke in the play, is to bear the part of an experienced and capable head of a city-state. His defeat of Hippolyta in battle marks his greatness as a warrior. His ability as judge is seen in his insistence upon the inviolability of the law and his efforts to avoid extreme penalty in yielding alternatives and time for reflection. His account of the life of a nun is vivid and picturesque. His philosophy is that it is better to suffer the trials of married life than to live in single blessedness. He is most courteous to Hippolyta and regardful of her, expressing his longing for her to become his wife, and apologizing for his lack of attention during his disposal of Egeus' appeal, even though he speaks of her indirectly as he delivers his sentence. He wishes to add to the happiness of her wedding day by providing entertainment.

HIPPOLYTA   She was the queen and leader in battle of a tribe of mythical women warriors supposed to live in Scythia, a country at the eastern end of the Black Sea. She speaks but once in the scene, remarking that the days and nights before the wedding day will pass quickly. Although she is colorless, she shows a touch of the romantic in her comparison of the moon bent to a silver bow. She acts on an equality with Theseus, and she has accepted his conquest of her in battle without complaint.

EGEUS   He is a typical citizen of Athens, probably of the noble class, since Hermia's two lovers are wealthy and well born. He is courteous to the duke and plain spoken. He lacks fatherly sympathy for his daughter, calling her stubborn and disobedient, and he thinks of no alternative but death if she refuses to submit to his will. He gives no reason for his choice of Demetrius and accuses Lysander of bewitching Hermia with songs and gifts.

DEMETRIUS   He speaks but two lines in the scene, appealing to Hermia for her love and demanding Lysander to yield his faulty claims. The duke calls him a worthy gentleman (nobleman); Lysander, comparing himself with him, acknowledges him to be of good birth and wealthy. Then in the same speech he calls him ''spotted and instant,'' and accuses him of unfaithfulness to Helena, whose soul he had won and then discarded.

LYSANDER   He appears much more attractive than Demetrius. Hermia states that he is as worthy a gentleman as Demetrius, and Lysander affirms that his birth is as good and his wealth, he thinks, is greater. He shows himself the true lover in his romantic wooing with poetry, music beneath her windows, bracelets of his hair, flowers and other fanciful gifts. His betrayal of Demetrius before the court is not to his credit, but lovers are excusable for unnatural behavior when their happiness is at stake. The incident is included to win the sympathy of the audience for Helena and to account for the later behavior of Demetrius.

When he and Hermia are left alone on the stage, he enters into her lyrical mood, but during his answers to her laments he is evidently thinking out his plan to elope. His quick resolve and his detailed explanation of how to solve their problem mark him as a resolute man of action. His ability in poetry, earlier charged as an accusation against him by Egeus, is well marked in his description of the moon to Helena, lines 209-213.

HERMIA Her first remarks show her a spirited woman. She bluntly tells Theseus that her lover is as worthy as Demetrius, and, turning to her father, she tells him that she wishes he had her eyes. She follows these retorts with demanding to know at once the worst that can follow her disobedience. She deliberately refuses before the duke to marry her father's choice, preferring to live and die a nun. In this she shows her self-assertion and defiance. Her father expresses the same qualities in her in terming her stubborn, harsh and disobedient.

When she is alone with Lysander, she becomes a typically romantic, distressed woman in seemingly hopeless love. Instead of breaking down in tears or passionately attacking her father and the duke for their hard-heartedness, as we might expect after the spirit she has shown, she engages with Lysander in an interchange of lyrical laments illustrating how "the course of true love never did run smooth." When Lysander answers with his plan of elopement, after she has concluded that they must resign themselves to fate, her spirits rebound into a song of lovers' oaths of her fidelity to keep tryst with him.

When Helena enters, she is herself again and speaks in more hopeful poetry. She proves to her friend her innocence in drawing the attentions of Demetrius by telling how she has tried to drive him from her and her purpose to leave Athens with Lysander. To convince her of her sincerity, she names the exact time and place where they are to meet.

HELENA Her sorrow over her lost lover leaves her disconsolate and helpless. Her nature, gentler than Hermia's, knows little of fight. Where Hermia uses frowns, curses, and hate – and we believe her an expert in them – Helena's weapons are smiles and beseechings. She is envious of Hermia's fascinating charms, and it is because of the blindness of love that she lost the favor of Demetrius' eyes. Hermia philosophically accepts her tragedy as a decree of fate. Helena takes fate into her own hands in deliberately telling Demetrius of the elopement, which in all probability will bring Hermia back to Athens and make her own case hopeless. But she is so hungry for a moment's attention from him that she risks losing him altogether for a word of thanks from him. However, she again puts her trust in fate in following him to the wood, where at least she will see him again.

HELENA AND HERMIA We learn later in the play that Helena is tall and fair, while Hermia is short and dark. This scene tells us that the former is gentle in speech and the latter sharp tongued. Helena's beauty and graces make her the heroine of the two, if either may be considered such. Shakespeare was mindful of the tall and fair-complexioned Queen Elizabeth, who appreciated the compliment of making all heroines resemble her. It was quite satisfactory to make inferior characters short and dark in accord with her unfortunate cousin and rival, Mary, Queen of Scots, who had been put to death only eight years before the play was written. The same difference in characters appears in Portia and Nerissa in *The Merchant of Venice*, in Rosalind and Celia in *As You Like It*, and in Olivia and Maria in *Twelfth Night*.

ACT I · SCENE 2

This scene also takes place in Athens, but instead of at the Ducal Palace, we are now among working men. We are now introduced to the following Athenian tradesmen: Quince the Carpenter, Snug the Joiner, Bottom the Weaver, Flute the Bellows-mender, Snout the Tinker, and Starveling the Tailor.

COMMENT: *The name of each tradesman is suited to the work he does in some way, but the association is subtle enough not to seem artificial: these are real people with real names. Snug suits a joiner, and Snout, as a tinker, mends kettles with spouts. A flute is a wind instrument and so is a, bellows, and tailors are traditionally undernourished. Quince is the name of a carpenter's tool, and a "bottom" is another name for a spool of thread, and therefore associated with a weaver. However, as William Hazlitt pointed out admiringly, the names of the tradesmen please us most because we feel that they are natural and that it is just luck that they characterize each trade so well. Bottom's name and occupation have a further significance which we shall note as the play progresses.*

These amiable, simple men have come together to prepare a play to be performed at the wedding of Theseus and Hippolyta. Quince is in charge and he begins by asking if all are present. Bottom, who is the most energetic participator, advises that Quince announce the name of the play and then call each man's name. Their play is, "The most lamentable comedy and most cruel death of Pyramus and Thisbe."

COMMENT: *The story of Pyramus and Thisbe was a popular tale of tragic love available to the Elizabethan in many forms and very familiar to Shakespeare's public. It concerns the traditional situation of lovers whose parents are enemies. Their secret meeting one moonlit night results in death for both, in a manner similar to that of Romeo and Juliet. The man, mistakenly thinking his lady is dead, kills himself; she, finding him dead, kills herself also. This theme is obviously related to the situation that has begun to unfold in the first scene concerning young love and its conflict with parental authority.*

Nick Bottom is the first name called, and Quince says he is to play Pyramus. Bottom asks, is Pyramus a lover or a tyrant? When he finds that Pyramus is a lover who kills himself for love, Bottom declares his fitness for the part, though his "chief humor" is to play a tyrant. He gives vigorous example of his talent in the latter capacity, reciting a fiery speech impromptu.

COMMENT: *When Bottom speaks of his "chief humor," he means his inclination by temperament for the role of tyrant. The people of Shakespeare's time believed that the human body was made up chiefly of four fluids or "humors": phlegm, blood, choler, and melancholy (also called black choler). A person's disposition and his temporary state of mind were determined according to the relative proportions of these fluids in his body;*

consequently, a person was said to be phlegmatic, sanguine, choleric, or melancholy. We still use these words to describe temperaments, though we have long abandoned the physiological theory which gave rise to them. The chief humor of Bottom, as he sees himself, is choler. Bottom's claim to be able to perform well in "Ercles' vein, a tyrant's vein" is a reference to Hercules, which was a popular stock ranting role. Bottom himself best describes what "ranting" is: "a part to tear a cat in, to make all split." The speech he gives to display his talent for this kind of part does indeed "tear" and "split" with its grating alliterations and pouncing rhymes. The "Phibbus' car" mentioned in the speech means the chariot of Phoebus Apollo, the sun god. Hercules Furens, by Seneca, portrayed the stock ranting figure of Hercules, and the style of Bottom's speech here parodies early translations of Seneca. In addition, we know that there were two major styles of acting in the Elizabethan theater, an artificial style and a more natural one. From references throughout Shakespeare we know that he approved of the more natural style, and that he thought the other style pompous and bombastic. Therefore, here Shakespeare may be parodying also the artificial style of acting, which was prone to become "ranting."

After Bottom is named to play Pyramus, Quince names Francis Flute the bellows-mender to play Thisbe. Flute asks if Thisbe is "a wandering knight." Quince answers that Thisbe is the lady that Pyramus loves. Flute objects to playing a woman, saying that he has a beard coming. Quince says that doesn't matter for he shall wear a mask and speak in a falsetto.

COMMENT: *A wandering knight is a knight-errant, who, along with a lover and a tyrant, was a typical role of the time. All female parts were played by boy actors in the theater of Shakespeare's day. There were no women actors at all. When we consider what magnificent women Shakespeare has created in his plays, we realize what excellent actors these boys must have been. It is hard to imagine a boy playing Juliet or Cleopatra, but that was the case in the days when Shakespeare's plays were first performed before an audience of his contemporaries.*

Hearing that Thisbe will be played in a mask, Bottom says if he may wear a mask he would like to play Thisbe too. He says he will speak in a "monstrous little voice" and he gives an example of his prowess in this regard. Quince insists, however, that Bottom play Pyramus and Flute, Thisbe. Bottom is temporarily quieted and with an air of injured magnanimity he allows the casting to proceed. We shall see that he is only subdued for a moment. Quince then names Robin Starveling for Thisbe's mother, Tom Snout for Pyramus' father, and himself for Thisbe's father.

COMMENT: *The parents of Pyramus and Thisbe are mentioned in the source story, but they do not appear in the play as acted. When the time comes for these tradesmen to perform, we shall see that Quince, Starveling, and Snout have new parts.*

Finally, Quince names Snug the joiner for the lion's part. Snug inquires if Quince has the lion's part written out, because if so, Snug would like to begin studying it. He is "slow of study" and wants to be sure to know it on time. Quince assures him that he may do it extempore, for all he has to do is roar. When he hears this, the irrepressible Bottom can no longer contain himself. He has been quiet for all of eleven lines, but the prospect of roaring is too much for him. He must chime in again: "Let me play the lion too." He enthusiastically describes how well he would roar. It will do people good to hear him and the Duke will request an encore. Quince and the others agree that to roar "too terribly" might frighten the Duchess and the ladies, causing them to shriek, and they would all be hanged for it. Bottom won't be stopped. First, he has a joke on the subject – if the ladies are frightened out of their wits, then they may be so foolish (being witless) as to hang them. Second, he has the necessary modification all ready. He will roar as gently as a dove or a nightingale.

COMMENT: *The lover and the tyrant whom Bottom could undertake equally well, are the same kind of direct opposites as a dove and a nightingale on the one hand, which are birds of love, and a lion on the other hand, fierce and savage king of the beasts. Thus Bottom is ready to take on anything. He has complete confidence in his ability to sweep thus from one end of the emotional scale to the other. Bottom the weaver is one of Shakespeare's most extraordinary creations. The energy and enthusiasm with which he partici- pates in life are immediately evident. Some critics have objected to what they consider his domineering, brash, self-centered personality, but this is a gross misunderstanding. His eagerness and vitality evince a love of life and a willingness to engage in it to his fullest capacity. Such a man cannot help but win our affection as we shall see he has won that of his comrades. We shall see that his talent for life, the beauty of his fresh, naïve eagerness will win for him a special place in this play where love and art and dreams assert their power over life. Bottom, the fundamental realist his name implies, will feel the power they assert most profoundly. His glory will be that starting from his position as a rock-bottom realist he can, with the same vigor and joy he brings to whatever he does, respond to his power and believe. The energy of his love of life unifies experience, and he is a weaver in this deeper sense too, as shall be seen.*

Despite the adroitness of Bottom's bid to play the Lion too, Quince insists he can play no part but Pyramus, persuasively citing as reasons that Pyramus is "sweet-faced," handsome ("proper"), and "a most lovely gentlemanlike man." Therefore, says the clever Quince, Bottom *has* to play Pyramus. Bottom at long last deigns to accept only the one role, little enough for his talents albeit the best part in the play. Having watched his virtuoso performance in this scene, we must share his self-estimate. Once his part has been narrowed to one, Bottom immediately opens up possibilities within it. He asks Quince what color beard he ought to wear and when Quince leaves it up to him, Bottom recites with great relish all the possible colors in beards:

"straw-color," "orange-tawny," "purple-in-grain" or- "French-crown-color beard, your perfit yellow." Thus he has already embarked with gusto on his theatrical venture. Quince makes a joke on "French-crown-color" saying that some French crowns have no hair at all and then Bottom would be playing bare-faced. Quince hands out the scripts and tells his actors to learn them for a rehearsal the next night. They are to meet in the palace wood a mile outside of town by moonlight. There, Quince states, they will have the privacy and secrecy not possible if they were to meet in the city.

In the meantime, Quince will assemble the necessary properties. Bottom agrees to this on behalf of everybody, saying, "there we may rehearse most obscenely and courageously." His excitement at the prospect carries him away and he uses the wrong word. Quince specifies the meeting place as the Duke's Oak. Naturally it is Bottom who has the last words in the scene as with sporting verve but only hazy meaning he says, "Enough. Hold, or cut bowstrings." We gather the meaning by the energy of the words, but we can only guess at their precise definition.

COMMENT: *It has been pointed out that Bottom's occupation as a weaver would make him particularly well-acquainted with various dyes. Also, costumes in the theater of Shakespeare's time were extremely elaborate, and actors in general would be greatly concerned with their apparel for a part. By French-crown-color, Bottom means the golden color of the French coin. The joke that Quince makes about this is because syphilis was called the French disease (every country blamed it on another – in France it was called the English disease), and he is saying that the heads ("crowns") of those with the French disease are bald. Bottom's use of words in the foregoing scene is comically inept, but through the sheer force of his personality he gets his meaning across. Perhaps he uses the word "obscenely" because it includes the word "scene" and he thinks it means something like putting forth a scene. His last words seem to be an archer's expression, probably meaning, "keep your promises or give up the play." A reference to archery is not out of keeping with this play. Hippolyta, who, as an Amazon, would be an excellent archer, describes the moon as a silver bow in Scene 1. Cupid's bow and arrow will be important later. Therefore, Bottom's ineptitude manages somehow to be meaningful. Finally, it should be noted that this scene is in prose and is meant to contrast with the formal poetry of the lover in Scene 1. Prose is often used in Shakespeare for characters who contribute realistic, down-to-earth comedy to a play.*

Notes

The following should be noted about the foregoing scene:

1. We are introduced to characters who are very, very different from those we met in Scene 1. This difference is expressed markedly by their language. The characters in this scene speak in the prose of comic realism, which contrasts with the formal poetry the lovers speak.

2.   However, connections between these two distinctly different groups have been established in three important ways:

(a)   The reason these men are preparing a play is to entertain at that same wedding of Theseus and Hippolyta discussed in Scene 1, at which Hermia must announce her decision.

(b)   The subject of the play they have chosen, while comically distant from their own world, is relevant to Hermia's plight.

(c)   Their plan to rehearse the next night in the Duke's wood a mile out of town by moonlight brings them into the same geographical area as the lovers who also plan to meet there. We can expect plot development from the physical proximity of these otherwise entirely separate worlds. In other words, we should be alerted that Shakespeare has brought the two different groups into the same woods for some plot reason.

ACT II · SCENE 1

This scene takes place in that wood near Athens which has been designated as a meeting place for the characters in each of the two preceding scenes. Puck or Robin Goodfellow and a Fairy enter from opposite sides. Puck inquires about the fairy's activities. The spirit answers in light and airy song, describing how he wanders everywhere more swiftly than the moon. He serves the Fairy Queen by taking care of the flowers which he calls her "pensioners" (members of the royal bodyguard in splendid uniforms). Specifically, he hangs dewdrops on the gold and ruby-spotted cowslips. The fairy bids farewell to Puck, saying the Queen and all her elves will come there soon. Puck says the King of the Fairies, Oberon, plans to be there also, and he warns the fairy to keep the Queen out of the King's sight, because King Oberon is very angry at his Queen. Queen Titania has a changeling, a lovely boy stolen from an Indian King, and Oberon is jealous and wants the child for his own. Titania not only withholds the changeling, but makes the little boy her special favorite. And so, Puck continues, every time Oberon and Titania meet, whether in wood or meadow, by a spring or under the stars, they quarrel so fiercely that all their elves are frightened and crawl into acorn cups to hide.

COMMENT: *The fairies in* A Midsummer Night's Dream *are Shakespeare's invention. There had, of course, been fairies in English folklore, but Shakespeare's differ in several important respects from these. It is Shakespeare's fairies as depicted here which have held sway over the public imagination ever since, replacing those of folk tradition. Shakespeare's differ from the latter in three outstanding ways: their diminutive size, their association with flowers, and their benevolent natures. The fairy of folklore had none of these characteristics. The Fairy's song with which the scene opens introduces still another kind of language into the play. Like that of the lovers and of the workmen, it expresses a different kind of character. It comes into being because this particular character requires it. The variety of language in this play, suitable to the kind of character who speaks it and serving to differentiate between characters, is one of Shakespeare's triumphs. We note, of course, the mention once again of the moon and flowers.*

After Puck's description of the frightened elves, so tiny that they can hide in acorn cups, the Fairy asks Puck if he is Robin Goodfellow. In asking the question, the Fairy describes some of the activities attributed to the elf Robin: frightening village maidens, skimming milk so it won't churn, taking the kick out of liquor, misleading people who travel at night, and for those who treat him well, doing work and bringing luck. Puck answers that he is the mischievous Robin Goodfellow, Hobgoblin, and Puck, and he recounts some more of his mischief. Besides being jester to King Oberon, he fools horses by neighing like a filly and he makes old women spill ale on themselves by getting into their cups in the shape of a "crab" and bobbing against their lips. Sometimes he pretends he's a three-foot stool and when a wise, old woman, in the middle of a sad tale, tries to sit down, he moves, she falls, crying "tailor" and coughing, and everybody laughs uproariously.

COMMENT: *Puck is a general name for mischievous devils or imps, but here is Robin Goodfellow, a household elf common in country folklore. The pranks Shakespeare credits him with here are homespun, domestic mischief, rich in colorful associations with English rural life. As well as doing all kinds of naughty tricks, Puck could be very helpful and do useful household tasks if so inclined. "Hobgoblin" means Robin the goblin, because "Hob" is a country form of Robert or Robin. A "crab" is a crab apple. The cry of the old woman, "tailor," means either one with a tail or refers to the fact that tailors sit on the floor.*

Puck concludes his speech with the announcement that Oberon is approaching. The Fairy says so is his mistress, Titania and he wishes Oberon were gone. At this point, the King of Fairies, Oberon, enters with his train at one door and the Queen, Titania, enters with her train at another. Oberon addresses Titania as "proud Titania" and calls their moonlight meeting unfortunate. She replies by calling him "jealous Oberon," and starts to leave, saying she has forsworn his bed and company. Oberon calls her a "rash wanton" (willful creature) and tells her to stay, reminding her that he is her lord. Titania replies that if he is her lord, she must be his lady. Then she begins reciting all his extracurricular romances as an ironical commentary on his claim to being her lord and master. She says he has stolen from fairyland and in the shape of the typical shepherd, Corin, he has played on pipes and sung love poetry to the shepherdess, Phillida. Titania continues by pointing out that he has come from faraway India only because Hippolyta is an old girlfriend who's getting married. The Queen's description of Hippolyta is finely sarcastic: "the bouncing Amazon,/Your buskined mistress and your warrior love." She closes by saying Oberon has come all that way to bless the marriage of Theseus and Hippolyta because he's sweet on the bride. Oberon immediately and indignantly rises in self-defense, saying Titania ought to be ashamed to bring that Hippolyta business up since he knows about *her* love for Theseus. Oberon then neatly rattles off the names of four women whom Theseus abandoned for Titania: the ravished Perigenia, Aegles, Ariadne, and Antiopa.

COMMENT: *When the King and Queen of the Fairies enter, they* *immediately address each other by name, thus informing the audience of their identity. Their feelings about each other are also skilfully communicated right away by Oberon's addressing Titania as "proud," and by her responding with "jealous Oberon." We not only learn who these characters are by these modes of address, but we learn what each thinks of the other. Accomplished in less than two lines, this is great dramatic economy. In one more line we learn another important piece of information. The result of the quarrel between them is that Titania has foresworn Oberon's bed and company. So again, the course of love is not running smoothly, only here we have a new variation of the same theme. The threat to Hermia is that she might have to foreswear forever what Titania chooses to give up here, while poor Helena has already had to do so against her will. In all three cases, love matters certainly need straightening out. Corin and Phillida are typical names for a shepherd and shepherdess in pastoral poetry (poetry dealing with rural life). The pipes of corn she accuses him of playing on are pipes made of grain stalks, usually oats. Buskins are a kind of leather legging. Perigenia is the Pergouna of Plutarch's account, one of Theseus' several mistresses. Aegles is North's spelling of Aegle, another of Theseus' mistresses. Ariadne was the daughter of Minos of Crete. She helped Theseus thread the labyrinth to kill the Minotaur and was abandoned by him on the island of Naxos when he returned to Athens. Antiopa is another name for Hippolyta, the Amazonian queen conquered by Theseus.*

Titania replies to this onslaught of her past amours with Theseus by accusing Oberon of making them up out of jealousy. She goes on to say that never, since the beginning of midsummer, has she been free of his brawling. Wherever they meet – hill, dale, forest, meadow, fountain, brook or seashore – he disturbs their merrymaking, as they dance with the wind in their hair. Therefore, she continues, since they piped music for the fairy dancing all in vain, the winds took revenge by sucking up contagious fogs from the sea and bringing them to land with disastrous results. These fogs have caused even "pelting" (paltry) rivers to overflow their banks. The resultant flooding has meant wasted labor for both the ox in the yoke and the ploughman driving him. The corn in these flooded fields has rotted while still green and immature. The pens where sheep and cattle should be, stand empty mid the general devastation, and the crows grow fat on the livestock dead of the murrain disease. The areas set aside for outdoor games, such as the nine men's morris (a game played on squares cut in the turf with counters such as pebbles or pegs), or the mazes, are filled with mud and indistinguishable from lack of use.

Titania continues that though men have all the hardships of that season, they have none of the comforts and compensations of winter, no hymns or carols bless the night. Because of Oberon's quarrel with her, says Titania, the moon, who is in control of floods, is pale with anger and keeps the whole atmosphere so drenched that "rheumatic diseases" (colds, grippe, rheumatism) are very prevalent. And as a result of the the foregoing disorder in nature ("distemperature"), the seasons are all mixed up. Frosts kill new roses, buds follow fast upon wintry days, none of the seasons act the way they are supposed to. People, watching in amazement for the usual indications for each season don't know which is which. Titania concludes by repeating that this string of evil consequences can be traced directly to their quarrel as its cause and origin. They "are the parents and the original" of this evil offspring.

COMMENT: *This famous passage about the weather is thought to be an allusion to the very bad weather of March, 1594, in England. This is significant because it is used as evidence for dating the play. If Titania is describing weather that prevailed in March, 1594, then* A Midsummer Night's Dream *must have been written after that date. Other information is used to ascertain a date* before *which it probably had to be written, so that scholars arrive at the date 1595-96 for the composition of this play.*

We should note that marital discord is here made responsible for violent disorder in the natural world. So we are still on the subject of love problems. The recitation of old romances with which each upbraided the other also serves to remind us of the problems of Hermia and Helena. Even these superior beings, the King and Queen of Fairyland, whose quarrels change the order of the seasons, are subject to the same vagaries in love. And by their mention of dealings with Theseus and Hippolyta, these latter lofty personages are also seen to be not too high for love's ups and downs. Thus, the Fairy Kingdom, though inhabited by very different creatures, has strong connections with the worlds we have already met. Not only does dissension in its royal household spoil the weather that men must experience, but there also has been involvement on an individual basis. Therefore, we can look for further developments along the lines of a connection between the fairy world and the mortal one.

The way in which Titania concludes her speech reminds us most strongly that the theme of love and marriage is the basis for this play. She says they are the parents of evil offspring – that is, since she has foresworn his bed and company, they do not produce children as would be the case were there marital harmony. Also, the amazed confusion of people who "know not which is which" when the seasons are all changed around is a significant description of the disorders and confusions caused by love problems. We should keep this phrasing in mind when future developments complicate our plot.

Oberon's answer to all of this is that the solution lies with Titania. There's no reason at all for her to quarrel with him. After all, he *just* wants a little changeling boy to be his "henchman" (page). His wheedling doesn't soften Titania, however. In her most queenly manner she denies him once again: "Set your heart at rest./The fairyland buys not the child of me." Then she explains how she got the boy. His mother was a "vot'ress" (had taken a vow) in the order of which Titania was patroness. They used to sit together on the yellow seashore and gossip. They would watch the trading ships sail out to sea and laugh when the wind made the canvas billow. Being pregnant with this boy, Titania's friend would imitate the ships and go fetch things from inland for Titania. She, being mortal, died giving birth to that boy, says Titania. And for her sake the Queen is bringing him up, and for her sake she will not part with him. After this moving and well-spoken explanation, Oberon asks only how long Titania plans to stay in that wood. Titania replies that she will probably stay till after Theseus is married. The Queen says if Oberon will be patient and participate harmoniously in her activities he should come with her. If not, then he ought to avoid her and she will do likewise. The stubborn King has only one objective. He will go with her if she will give him the boy. But Titania is of an equally firm disposition and she retorts, "Not for thy fairy kingdom." She bids her fairies away, saying she'll only quarrel more if she stays longer. With haughty splendor, she and her train leave. Oberon and Puck are now left to confer on the situation.

Oberon says to the departed Queen, well, if that's the way she wants it. Then he vows that before she leaves that wood, he'll torment her for the injury he considers she has done him. At this point he calls Puck to him. Oberon tells him to recall on occasion when the King sat on a promontory and heard a mermaid's song. His description is a high point in this play's poetry: the mermaid is on a dolphin's back, and she is "Uttering such dulcet and harmonious breath/That the rude sea grew civil at her song,/And certain stars shot madly from their spheres/To hear the sea-maid's music." Puck replies that he remembers the incident. Oberon goes on to say that at that time he saw, though Puck could not, armed Cupid flying between the moon and the earth. Cupid took aim at "a fair vestal, throned by the west." He missed this target however. Oberon saw him shoot the love-arrow from his bow with the force to pierce a multitude of hearts. But the Fairy King could also see that the fiery shaft was "Quenched in the chaste beams of the wat'ry moon," missing the "imperial vot'ress," who went her way "In maiden meditation, fancy-free." Oberon saw where Cupid's arrow did fall. It hit "a little western flower," which had been white but after being hit turned purple. The name of this flower among maidens is "love-in-idleness." Oberon tells Puck to go out and get that flower for him, the one he once showed to him. The King explains that the juice of this flower, when put on the sleeping eyelids of man or woman, will cause the person to fall madly in love with the very first live creature that is seen upon waking, no matter who or what. Oberon repeats his instruction that Puck get this herb, saying the spirit should be back in less time than it takes a whale to swim a league. Puck replies that he will encircle the earth in forty minutes, and leaves to get the little flower. Oberon, left alone, announces his intention in a soliloquy. Once he has this juice, he'll wait for an opportunity to put some on Titania's eyelids while she sleeps. Then, the very first thing she sees when she wakes – whether it's a lion, bear, wolf, bull, monkey, or ape – she shall be madly in love with to the depths of her soul. While she is in this condition of only having eyes for this creature, Oberon will be able to get the little changeling from her. Afterwards, when he has accomplished this goal, he can take the charm off her sight with another herb.

COMMENT: *We should note first of all the great beauty of the poetry that Oberon and Titania speak. Oberon's speech about the beautiful music calming the sea and causing the stars to fall contributes to the whole statement this play is making about the power of art over life, and the important relation between love, art, beauty, "illusion" on the one hand and life, nature, "reality" on the other hand. Reality cannot exclude the former terms.*

The "fair vestal" and "imperial vot'ress" is Queen Elizabeth of England (throned by the West) who never married. In this allusion, the Virgin Queen is described as a votaress of Diana, the virgin moon-goddess. A vestal is a virgin priestess. "Fancy-free" means free of love thoughts. "Love-in-idleness" is another name for the pansy. The change from white to purple described in these lines may have been suggested by the change of the mulberries in the same way by the blood of Pyramus in Ovid's Metamorphoses *(iv. 125-27).*

Critics think that the imagery in this passage is reminiscent of an entertainment put on for Queen Elizabeth. Two entertainments have been suggested, either the one at Kenilworth in 1575 or that at Elvetham in 1591. The noted authority, Sir William Chambers, favors Elvetham, although he points out that all these pageants were very similar and that the special feature of a mermaid on a dolphin was not at either.

We should take note of how this play's special motifs, which we have pointed out and drawn attention to all along, appear all together in this crucial passage. First, the flower is hit by an arrow from Cupid's bow. Bows and arrows were mentioned previously.

The moon is an important presence in the scene. It is mentioned twice and has the special office of protecting the vestal maiden from Cupid's arrow by quenching the fiery shaft. Furthermore, we have remarked previous mentions of flowers and here the juice of a flower is given significant power. Also, transformation was discussed earlier, and here the imperial vot'ress escapes the love metamorphosis, but the flower's resultant transformation is the cause of its power. Finally, this power that Oberon plans to use on Titania is of special significance. It rests on terms that have been previously and firmly established in the play: this juice affects the eyesight *and controls one's* vision *of love. When these terms came up in combination earlier in our text, they were duly emphasized and should be recalled now that they re-enter here.*

The combination of all these things prepares us for the importance that this love-juice does indeed have in our plot. Arrow, moon, flower, transformation, eyesight, are all signposts telling us to be alert for developments arising from what Oberon is starting here with this magic potion. And the very next thing that happens shows us we are not going to be disappointed.

As soon as Oberon finishes explaining his plan to use the love-juice on Titania, he notices two people approaching and wonders who they are. He declares that he will become invisible so that he can overhear their conversation. The two people are none other than Demetrius and Helena, who now enter with her following him. Demetrius is avowing that he does not love

Helena and that she ought not to pursue him therefore. He wants to know where Lysander and Hermia are. Recall that Helena has told him of the planned elopement. He reminds Helena that she told him they had stolen into this wood, "And," he says, "here am I, and wood within this wood," because he cannot find Hermia. (Wood means mad.) Demetrius concludes by brusquely ordering Helena off, telling her to follow him no more. Helena answers that he is like a magnet that draws her to him, except that her heart is not iron but steel, which is truer. She says if he'll stop having such magnetism, she'll stop following him. Demetrius asks if he entices her or speaks persuasively, then answers his own rhetorical questions by saying that he has told her straight out that he does not and cannot love her. Helena says she only loves him the more for that. She likens herself to the spaniel, which fawns on him the more he beats her. She asks that he use her only as a spaniel – spurn, strike, neglect, or lose her – only allow unworthy Helena to follow him. She says that's the lowest place she can ask for, to be used as his dog, but high enough for her. Demetrius warns her not to arouse too much hatred in him, and adds that it makes him sick to look at her. All Helena says to such abuse is that it makes her sick *not* to look at him. Then Demetrius points out the immodesty of her following him, leaving the city and putting herself at the mercy of someone who doesn't love her, when the darkness and the seclusion increase the threat to her virginity. Helena replies that his virtue is her protection, that his face lights the night for her, that he is all the world to her so she's not alone.

Demetrius says he'll run and hide, leaving her to the mercy of the wild beasts. She says he may do so, for he is worse than they could be. She adds that all tales of pursuit shall be turned around and the pursuer shall become the pursued – Daphne chase Apollo, the dove chase the griffin, the hind pursue the tiger – and how ridiculous is such a chase where cowardice pursues and valor flies. Demetrius says he won't listen any more, and if she continues to follow him, he warns that he will do some mischief to her in the wood. Helena agrees ironically, saying he does her mischief everywhere: temple, town, field. She concludes by calling his behavior scandalous, since he reverses the role of the sexes, making her do the wooing. Demetrius exits as Helena says, "We should be wooed, and were not made to woo." Then Helena herself leaves, saying she will follow him and that to die at his hand would be making a heaven of hell.

Oberon, who has been observing all that has passed between Demetrius and Helena, now says he will reverse that situation. Before Demetrius leaves the wood, she will flee from him and he will pursue her. At this point, Puck enters, and Oberon asks if he has the flower with him and welcomes him back. Puck says he has it. Oberon asks him for it. Here follows another of the play's noteworthy passages of poetry. Oberon describes the place where Titania sleeps – "I know a bank where the wild thyme blows" – and he names all the flowers that surround her. He adds that there also the snake sheds her skin, a garment big enough for a fairy's outfit. While Titania sleeps there, Oberon will put this juice on her eyes, which will make her "full of hateful fantasies." Oberon then tells Puck to take some juice too, and go looking through the woods for a couple of Athenians. The lady is in love and the youth disdains her, and so, says Oberon, anoint the youth's eyes when the next thing he sees is the lady. Oberon tells Puck he may recognize the youth by his Athenian clothes. He instructs his spirit to be especially careful so that the youth may be more in love with the lady than she with him. Oberon's concluding words instruct Puck to meet him before the cock crows. Puck's reassurance that he will do so closes this scene.

COMMENT: *When Oberon declares, "I am invisible," he is entitled by Elizabethan stage convention to remain on the stage without being seen by any other characters who may enter. Sometimes a character would put on a black cloak and by this the audience was to understand that he could not be seen by other people on stage.*

When Demetrius says he is wood in the wood, he begins a series of puns on the locale of the play, which is added to by Helena at line 242 when she says women should be wooed. Wood meaning forest, wood meaning mad, and woo'd or wooed meaning courted are meaningfully connected in this play.

Helena's remarks on the lowly place of the spaniel and their abject servility should be noted because of Shakespeare's repeated reference to these animals in this way. When Helena speaks of traditional pursuit stories being turned around, we have another instance of the transformation theme. Daphne fled from Apollo and was changed into a laurel tree. The griffin is a mythical beast with the head of an eagle and the body of a lion. A hind is a doe. Reversing the role of the sexes and changing hell into heaven are remarks of Helena which also serve to recall the play's concern with the theme of transformation. Oberon's concluding speech names six different flowers just for the pleasure of recounting them: thyme, oxslip, violet, woodbine, musk-rose, and eglantine. All this is not needed for a mere identification of Titania's bower. The snake-skin big enough for a fairy is a colorful detail serving to remind us of the diminutive size of these creatures. By the end of the speech we see how the affairs of the fairies are going to have a bearing on the lovers.

Notes

In this scene we learn of the quarrel between Oberon and Titania. The plot of the former for the latter begins to weave in with the predicament of the lovers, because Oberon witnesses Helena's one-sided affection and determines to remedy this. The following should be noted about this scene:

1.   Oberon and Titania speak poetry of great beauty. Puck's poetry is remarkable for rough vigor and a rustic flavor all its own. It contrasts with the delicacy of the fairy songs. When Demetrius and Helena enter they are still speaking in the uninteresting, wooden way we have already seen. This contrasts markedly with the flexibility and grace of the poetry given to the fairies.

2.   The scene opens and closes with a speech about flowers. At least nine different flowers are mentioned in this scene alone: pansy ("little western

flower''), cowslip, rose, wild thyme, oxslip, violet, woodbine, musk-rose, eglantine.

3.   There have been a multitude of references to the theme of change and transformation. The following major instances ought to be remembered:

(a)   The quarrel between Oberon and Titania is over a "changeling."

(b)   Not only the cause but the result of the quarrel concerns change – the seasons have become all turned around.

(c)   The solution to the quarrel is possible because of a change in a little flower that occurred at the same time that the Virgin Queen did not change.

(d)   The power of this changed flower is to transform love-sight.

In general, the moon, which presides over the whole play, is constantly changing from one phase to another. Both love and art look to the moon as their sovereign star. Art transforms reality. And we have been told over and over that love has to do not with constancy but with change.

ACT II • SCENE 2

This scene takes place in another part of the woods. Titania enters with her attendants. She bids them dance and sing and then go perform their various duties. Some will kill worms ("cankers") in flowers, some will fight with bats ("reremice") for their wings out of which elves' coats shall be made, some will keep back the noisy owl that nightly hoots at them. First they must sing her asleep, then do the above jobs. The fairies then sing their song. It is a lullaby, consisting of two four-line tetrameter stanzas and a six-line chorus. In it, snakes, hedgehogs, newts, and blindworms (small snakes) are told not to come near the Fairy Queen. Then the chorus calls on Philomele, the nightingale, to come and sing in this lullaby for the Queen. The closing lines of the chorus ask that no harm, spell or charm, come near the lovely Titania. The second stanza warns off spiders, beetles, worms, and snails, and is followed by the same chorus as above.

During the second chorus, Titania falls asleep. The fairies depart to perform the tasks she assigned, leaving one of their band as sentinel. When they have left, Oberon enters and squeezes the flower which Puck brought to him on Titania's eyelids. The King incants a charm over her while doing this. Like the fairies' lullaby, it is in rhymed tetrameter lines. It says that whatever she sees upon waking she will fall in love with, whether ounce (lynx), cat, bear, pard (leopard), or bristly boar. No matter what it is, in her eyes it will appear beloved, and Oberon concludes by wishing she wake when some vile thing is near. Then he exits.

COMMENT: *All of the poetry is in the uniquely light and graceful style created by Shakespeare to express the nature of these special creatures. The duties that Titania details to her crew add to our information about this fairy world. Using bats' wings for elves' coats emphasizes once again their small size. The fairies' lullaby specifically tries to ward off spells and charms, but the very next thing that happens is Oberon's putting a charm on Titania.*

The lullaby names eight small animals and insects, plus the nightingale. Oberon's incantation over the sleeping Titania, when he puts the love-juice on her eyes, adds six large animals to this list. The former song asks that nothing come near the Queen; the latter song asks that something does come near, the viler the better. The approach of humans is not covered by either song.

After Oberon has left Titania sleeping with the love-juice on her eyelids, Lysander and Hermia enter. They are trying to execute their plan to elope to Lysander's aunt's house. Lysander speaks, remarking that Hermia is weak from wandering in the woods and admits that he has forgotten how to get to their destination. He suggests that if Hermia is agreeable, they'll rest where they are and await daylight. Hermia agrees, says she will rest right there and he ought to go look for a place for himself. Lysander suggests that they sleep on the same turf since their hearts are betrothed to each other. Hermia says no to this, telling him twice to lie further off. Lysander says his intentions are pure and innocent and then he speaks of how their two hearts are really one so she ought not to deny him a sleeping place at her side. Lying thus, he does not lie, says Lysander. Hermia compliments him on his riddling and says she never meant to accuse him of being a liar, but she still insists that he lie further off for modesty's sake. She wants enough space left between them, as society deems proper between a bachelor and a maid. She bids him good night and wishes his love never alter till the end of his life. Lysander adds Amen to that, saying may his life end when his loyalty to her does. He lies down and prays that sleep come to her. Hermia wishes him the same and they both sleep.

COMMENT: *We have been expecting Hermia and Lysander to put in an appearance because (a) we knew they planned to meet in the wood to embark on their elopement and (b) we saw Demetrius and Helena at the end of the last scene and Demetrius spoke of the elopement, demanding of Helena the whereabouts of Lysander and Hermia. One would have expected Lysander to lose the way to auntie's house. Not only is it a stock fairy-tale plot complication, but also Lysander does not inspire one with confidence in his ability. His riddling and smooth-talking here show him to be a rather silly and shallow youth, harmless enough but withal a fatuous nonentity in terms of dramatic characterization. Note the confident assertions of unaltered loyalty to his love, Hermia. Hermia hopes he'll love her till he dies. Lysander takes this statement and goes right out on a limb with it, saying he hopes to die when he ceases to love her.*

While Hermia and Lysander lie asleep, Puck enters. Recall that Oberon had given him some love-juice to remedy the situation Helena was in with the unloving Demetrius, which the King witnessed. He told Puck to look for a youth with Athenian garments on and put the charm on him. Now Puck says he has gone through the forest without being able to find this Athenian to put the magic juice on. Then he spies Lysander and sees his Athenian clothes. He shouts with joy at gaining the object of his search, saying this must be whom Oberon meant, the Athenian youth who despises the maid. Then he sees

Hermia, assuming she is the suffering maiden, and remarking how she dare not lie close to this nasty man – this "lack-love," "kill-courtesy," "churl" (boor). Consequently, Puck casts all the power of the love-charm on Lysander, bidding love take over his eyes and that he wake when Puck is gone. The spirit departs to rejoin Oberon. As soon as he has left, Demetrius and Helena enter at a run. She is begging him to stay, even though he kill her. He bids her be off and stop haunting him. She begs him not to leave her in the dark thus. But Demetrius leaves alone, threatening her with peril if she doesn't stay where she is.

Helena is now by herself and she says she is out of breath with this foolish pursuit, and the more she prays the less she gets. She compares herself to Hermia, happy wherever she may be, and speaks of the beauty of her eyes in particular. Helena says that tears did not make Hermia's eyes so bright because her own are more often washed that way. She says she is as ugly as a bear and it's no wonder that Demetrius flees from her, since all the beasts do. It was absurd of her to compare her eyes to Hermia's. At this point Helena sees Lysander on the ground. She cannot tell if he be dead or asleep and to find out, she awakens him. Of course, Lysander has the lovejuice on his eyes so when he awakens and sees Helena he immediately declares his great love for her. He says he will run through fire for her. He calls her "transparent Helena," saying he can see her heart through her bosom. He asks her where Demetrius is, calls him vile, and ends with the fiery statement that such a man is fit to die on his sword. Helena tells Lysander not to talk that way about Demetrius, even though the latter does love Hermia. For, says Helena, Hermia still loves Lysander and that should content him. Lysander forcefully denies that he could be content with Hermia. He says he repents the time he has spent with the latter; he loves Helena, not Hermia, having had the good sense to change a raven for a dove. He then dwells at length on how this change from one love to another is an instance of his reason governing his will. Reason has told him Helena is worthier, his reason was not ripe till now, but now that it is ripe it is governing his will. And *that's* why he loves Helena. His reason leads him to her eyes where he reads love's stories in love's richest book. Helena is quite taken aback by all this and she assumes that Lysander is making fun of her and scorning her. She asks, isn't it enough she has so much trouble with Demetrius, but he should thus torment her for her insufficiency. She says he does her great wrong to woo her thus in jest – she thought he was better bred than that. She says farewell, and leaves lamenting that she should be refused by one man and abused by another because of that refusal.

COMMENT: *Now things are really beginning to happen. Oberon's instructions to Puck did not take into account that there were two Athenian youths in the wood, and so his mode of identifying Demetrius was not sufficient. The big issue Hermia made over not sleeping too near Lysander is now seen to have important results:*

(a) Puck knows the youth he's looking for despises the maid who loves him. When he sees Lysander and Hermia lying at some distance from each

other, it is supporting evidence for his mistaken identification of the youth as Demetrius.

(b)   When Helena comes on the scene, she can awaken Lysander without awakening Hermia also. Thus Puck's mistake can have the outcome it does.

(c)   Since Helena does not see Hermia, she can't turn to her for an explanation. Furthermore, Hermia doesn't observe the situation either.

We should note the convenient coincidences that are operating here in that as soon as Lysander has been prepared and Puck has left, Demetrius and Helena appear. Then Helena is left alone to encounter Lysander alone. Neither Demetrius nor Hermia sees what happens. When Helena and Demetrius enter, even though they are running, and their words are very urgent indeed, the form they speak in is that very formal "stichomythia" explained earlier (characters speak single alternating lines that rhyme with each other two by two). When Demetrius leaves after four lines of this kind of alternating dialogue, Helena continues to speak of her woeful plight in rhymed couplets. This pretty formality casts the action into the proper key – this is not a stark tragedy but a romantic comedy. We should note that Helena dwells on the subject of eyes, comparing her own and Hermia's. A long list of animals entered our imagery earlier in this scene and here too a bear is mentioned when poor Helena says she must look like one. She mentions beasts and monsters also.

Her speaking in rhymed couplets is the source of great comedy when she awakens Lysander, because the last line of her speech begins a couplet that is finished by the extravagant avowal of love he pops out with as soon as he opens his eyes. Helena: "Lysander, if you live, good sir, awake." Lysander, starting up: "And run through fire I will for they sweet sake." The absurdity of this protestation is heightened by this trick with the rhyme. After all, the last thing Lysander said before dropping off to sleep was that he would die if ever he stopped loving Hermia. And here he is, making the most extravagant love vows to another girl, and rhyming them instantly at that. No matter if he's just been awakened from a deep sleep – this is like a musical comedy routine where, at the drop of a hat, everybody in sight suddenly performs synchronized dance-steps in harmonizing pastel costumes. And there is more comedy to come, for the enchanted Lysander now chooses to explain his actions as based on reason. While we know he is just a puppet on a string, he goes on and on about how his will is at last being properly governed by his mature reason. We laugh in the security of our superior knowledge, but we must reserve judgment until the play has completed its statement about love and judgment, will and reason, vision and eyesight, illusion and reality. We may still laugh at Lysander but we may also laugh at ourselves, knowing a little more because we have realized that we know a lot less.

Lysander compares Hermia to a raven and Helena to a dove. Hermia was played by a dark actor and Helena by a light. Future remarks will substantiate this and we will also be told that Helena is tall and Hermia short.

After Helena's departure, Lysander remarks that she has not seen Hermia. He bids Hermia stay sleeping where she is and he wishes she may never come near him. He likens her to a sweet food of which he has had a surfeit and to a false belief which is hated when no longer held. He says, may she be hated by all, but most of all by him. He concludes by vowing all his love and strength to the honor and protection of Helena, and then leaves. Hermia awakens when he has left and cries to him for help, asking him to pluck a serpent from her breast. She has had a dream that a serpent was eating her heart and that Lysander looked upon the cruelty with a smile. She is still quaking with fear. She calls his name twice, asks where he might be, bids him speak, and finally ascertaining that he is not anywhere near, she leaves to find him or to die if not.

COMMENT: *Lysander's words to Hermia are needlessly cruel and her terror when she wakes is justified by his behavior towards her, though its immediate cause is her bad dream. Her mention of a serpent continues the allusions to animals in this scene, as did Lysander's mention of a raven and a dove. With Hermia's exit here the merry chase is on: she is looking for Lysander who is pursuing Helena who is following Demetrius who is searching for Hermia.*

Notes

This scene has accomplished the following:

1.   Titania's eyes have been enchanted and she awaits being awakened by her destined "beloved."

2.   Puck has mistaken Lysander for Demetrius and has put the charm on him so that now Lysander loves Helena.

3.   The situation is now worsened from the beginning, because neither man loves the woman who loves him. Hermia loves Lysander who loves Helena who loves Demetrius who loves Hermia. The fairies dance their rounds and ringlets and roundels, and the lovers too prance unwittingly in a circle.

ACT III · SCENE 1

This scene takes place in the wood near Titania's bower. The Athenian workmen enter: Quince, Snug, Bottom, Flute, Snout, and Starveling. They have come to rehearse their play as they planned to do in Act I, Scene 2. Bottom is the first to speak and he asks if they are all present. Quince says yes and that the spot they're in is a good place for their rehearsal. It has a clear plot to serve as a stage, and a hawthorn hedge to serve as a dressing room. They will do it just as they intend to before the Duke. Bottom here addresses Quince, who turns his attention to his friend, "bully Bottom." Bottom wishes to call Quince's attention to certain things in their play which will never please its audience. First, Pyramus must kill himself with his sword – the ladies will not be able to stand that. Bottom wants to know what's to be done about it.

Snout agrees that it is a "parlous" (perilous, terrible) fear, and Starveling thinks they'll have to leave the killing out of the final production. But no, the resourceful Bottom has a ready solution. He says he must recite a prologue that explains everything: their swords do no harm, Pyramus is not dead really, and in fact Pyramus is really Bottom the Weaver. In short, the prologue must declare that all the make-believe is merely make-believe. Then, says Bottom, the audience will not be afraid. Quince agrees to such a prologue and suggests it be written in "eight and six" (lines of eight and six syllables alternating, which is the common ballad metre). Bottom cannot resist adding the last touch, so he says it should be written in eight-syllable lines entirely. Snout asks, won't the ladies be afraid of the lion. Starveling, for one, fears just that result. Bottom says very grandly that they ought to consider very carefully bringing in "a lion among ladies." He says, "there is not a more fearful wild-fowl than your lion living," and it requires some attention. Snout unoriginally suggests another prologue. But Bottom again comes up with the solution that works. The lion costume should not entirely conceal the actor wearing it and he must announce that the lion really isn't one, then say his name is Snug the joiner.

This plan Quince agrees to and he brings up two more production problems. Thisbe and Pyramus are supposed to meet by moonlight, and also they must talk through a wall. First moonlight is discussed. Snout asks if the moon shines the night of the play, and Bottom calls for an almanac to find out. Quince says, yes, it does. Bottom says then they may leave a window open during their performance and the moonlight will come into the chamber that way. Quince says yes to this idea, adding as an alternative that a man may present moonshine with a lantern and a thorn bush.

Then Quince states the second production problem: Pyramus and Thisbe are supposed to talk through a chink in a wall. Snout doesn't see how they can possibly satisfy this requirement and he asks Bottom's opinion. The indomitable Bottom has the answer. It is based on Quince's idea for moonshine – let a man with plaster, loam, or roughcast on him stand for a wall and he can hold his fingers up for Pyramus and Thisbe to talk through as a chink. Quince agrees that in such a fashion they may solve their production problems. He then begins the rehearsal, calling for Pyramus first. After speaking, everyone shall enter the hawthorn hedge on cue.

COMMENT: *The great pains that our simple workmen take to explain away every illusion offers another comment on the reality / illusion theme at the heart of this play. To these men, reality and illusion are two entirely separate entities, and they insist upon stating which is which at every point where the slightest confusion might arise. They take absolutely no chances on this question. The manner in which their production goes forward is a classic expression of the position they represent on this question.*

Their production difficulties concerning the moonshine that is required also serve to draw attention once again to this important ingredient in our play's magic. But we should notice that when Bottom and his fellows deal with the moon, even that evanescent, inconstant body is brought down to earth and made to conform to their no-nonsense realism. Better have one of their own company represent moon than leave the matter up to that fleeting, shifting natural phenomenon.

The reference to "a lion among ladies" is thought to refer to a royal baptismal celebration at which a lion was to have drawn a carriage in the procession. But a blackamoor had to be substituted because the ladies present were frightened. This similarity to a historical event is used as evidence in assigning a date to this play.

After Quince has explained the rehearsal procedure and called on Pyramus to begin, Puck enters. He wonders aloud, "What hempen homespuns have we swagg'ring here, / So near the cradle of the Fairy Queen?" He sees it is a play rehearsal and says he'll watch and perhaps act too if he sees the opportunity. He is not seen by anyone. Quince now directs Pyramus to speak and Thisbe to stand forth. In his first line, Pyramus (Bottom) says "odious" instead of "odors" and Quince corrects him. Bottom makes the correction incorrectly, and continues till he must exit to investigate a noise he hears. Puck comments on what a strange Pyramus Bottom makes and he exits too. Thisbe (Flute) asks if it is his turn to speak. Quince explains that it is, Pyramus having just gone to "see a noise that he heard" and that he will be back. Then Thisbe speaks, praising her Pyramus in flower terms and saying she will meet him at "Ninny's tomb." Quince corrects this to "Ninus' tomb," adding that Flute is not supposed to speak that yet – that's supposed to be in answer to Pyramus. Flute has spoken his part all at once, cues and all. Quince calls for Bottom to enter, saying his cue is past. Thisbe repeats Bottom's cue and at this point Pyramus re-enters and now he has the head of an ass in place of his human one. Puck accompanies him. Quince shouts out his dismay: "O monstrous! O strange! We are haunted." They all flee in terror from the transformed Bottom, leaving him alone. Puck leaves in order to further torment the terrorized tradesmen. The spirit says he'll assume various animal shapes – horse, hound, hog, headless bear, fire too – and lead the deranged Athenians a merry chase through bog, bush, brake, briar, while he makes all the appropriate animal sounds.

Left alone, Bottom, who does not realize what Puck has done to him, expresses his own amazement at the behavior of his fellows. Since he doesn't know his own condition, he wonders why they have run away from him. He decides that they are playing a practical joke on him and trying to make him afraid. Here Snout re-enters and exclaims, "O Bottom, thou art changed! what do I see on thee?" Bottom's answer is that Snout sees an ass-head of his own. Snout leaves and then Quince re-enters and exclaims in turn, "Bless thee, Bottom! bless thee! thou art translated." When Quince has left again and the bewildered Bottom is alone, he resolutely confronts his situation and analyzes thus: "I see their knavery: this is to make an ass of me; to fright me, if they could." He decides that he'll show them he's not afraid – he'll stay right where he is and not run after them. And furthermore, to show most plainly his courage in the face of adversity, he'll walk around and sing so they'll hear that he's not afraid.

COMMENT: *With Puck's chance entrance upon the workmen's rehearsal, the fairy plot begins to interweave with the workmen's affairs. In the preceding scene, the fairy world began affecting the lovers' affairs. We must watch the progressive interweaving of these threads. Notice how extensively flowers figure in the dialogue of "Pyramus and Thisbe." We have pointed out before how this is a continuing motif. Existing right alongside this element in the play's atmosphere is a very contrasting type of imagery: Puck's cataloguing of the animals he'll imitate to frighten the workmen and his graphic recital of the rough sound-effects with which he'll pursue them. We have pointed out this contrast between the delicacy and light airiness of the fairy language on the one hand and Puck's homey, rough style on the other.*

Ninus' tomb is the rendezvous of Pyramus and Thisbe in Ovid. Ninus was the mythical founder of Nineveh; his wife Semiramis was supposed to have built the wall of Babylon, at which place the scene of the story of Pyramus and Thisbe is laid. Quince's difficulty with his actors – that they speak everything together, cues and dialogue – is the classic problem of the director of amateur theatricals.

Bottom's transformation brings to a climax this important theme in the play, whose emergence we have noted in many places. His transformation will work together with the other climax of this theme – the transformation produced by the little western flower – to produce the play's complete statement about reality and illusion, life and love. When Snout and Quince use the words "changed" and "translated," we are meant to remember all the times, and they are many, that these words have appeared in our text. At the end of Act II, Scene 1, we summarized some of the major instances.

Bottom does not know that he has been given the head of an ass by Puck when he twice mentions being an ass. He is merely speaking metaphorically of his condition. Of course, our knowing position makes these comments of his very ironical.

Really frightened and bewildered, but resolutely disclaiming this, Bottom bravely "whistles in the dark" to keep his spirits up in the face of such perplexing behavior on the part of his companions. He therefore walks back and forth and sings a song about a "woosel cock," a "throstle," and a "wren with little quill." His singing wakes Titania, who has been sleeping nearby, and she says, "What angel wakes me from my flow'ry bed?" Bottom continues undaunted, singing another verse about several more birds: finch, sparrow, lark, and cuckoo. (The "plain-song" of the last is noticed by many and they cannot say "nay" to it). Bottom comments on this last fact in his song, saying it is indeed useless to refute a foolish bird, even though he may be wrong. Now Titania is awake, and with eyes enchanted by the love-juice, she has seen Bottom. Consequently she says will he please sing some more, for she loves to hear him. In fact, she continues, she loves to look at him also. Her words are ironical here, because she doesn't know how very true they are, but we do: "So is mine eye enthrallèd to thy shape," says the poor deluded Queen. To this "hempen homespun" crowned with the head of an ass, the Queen of Fairies says that his "fair virtue's force" (the compelling attraction of his manly charms) causes her on first sight to swear she loves him.

Bottom answers her with the same unswerving realism he applied to the last line of his song. He tells her with plain and beautiful truth that she has little reason for that avowal. He adds the comment that reason and love "keep little company together nowadays," and it's too bad they don't get together. He comments on this observation, saying that he can "gleek" sometimes (make biting jests). Titania's response exhibits the superfluity of her passion – "Thou art as wise as thou art beautiful," she proclaims. Her excessiveness contrast with Bottom's true and solid declarations, and he himself catches her up on this foolishness, saying abruptly, "Not so." But, he adds, if he were wise enough to get out of the wood, that would be wise enough for him. Now the Queen in Titania reasserts herself, as she says with all the authority of her high position, "Out of this wood do not desire to go." She tells Bottom that he will stay whether he wants to or not, and she explains that she is a powerful spirit on whose commands the summer itself depends. And she loves him. Thus he will go with her and she will have fairies wait upon him. Bottom will sleep on flowers while they sing, and, she concludes, she will "purge thy mortal grossness so" that Bottom will become like an airy spirit. At this point she calls her four fairies to attend on Bottom: Peaseblossom, Cobweb, Moth, and Mustardseed.

COMMENT: *A "woosel" or ouzel is the English blackbird or merle, of the thrush family. A "throstle" is a song thrush or marvis. A "quill" is a pipe made of a reed or stalk and here refers to the wren's song. "Plain-song" means a simple and unvarying song. In the case of the cuckoo, this sounds like cuckold, so many a man hearing this applied to him cannot deny it.*

We should note that Bottom's remarks on reason and love are very correct statements of what happens in this play. Saying that he would be sufficiently wise if he had wit enough to get out of this wood is a clever statement because wood also means mad, as was pointed out earlier.

When Puck came in and announced that Bottom and his fellows were near the bower of Titania, the plot development became obvious. But no matter if the coincidence is extravagant, the sight of Titania in love with the ass-headed Bottom loses none of its effect. The names of the fairies that Titania calls are in keeping with the tiny, airy, delicate creatures Shakespeare has created in this play.

The four fairies enter at Titania's call and each in turn announces that he is ready, then in chorus ask where she wants them to go. Titania then lists all the services she wants them to perform for her beloved Bottom. They must accompany him courteously and kindly, feeding him with fruits – apricots, dewberries, purple grapes, green figs, and mulberries. They should steal honey from the bumblebees for him, and to light his way at night they will ignite torches from the glow-worm's eyes. She instructs them to pluck butterfly's wings to fan the moonbeams from his eyes as he sleeps. At her behest, each fairy says, "Hail, mortal!" Bottom genteely returns the greeting and courteously inquires each elf's name. He has a friendly comment upon each name. To Cobweb he says he will use him if he cuts his finger (cobweb was used to staunch blood). To Peaseblossom he says he wishes to be commended to Mistress Squash, his mother, and to Master Peascod, his father (a squash is an unripe pea pod and a peascod is a ripe pea pod). To Mustardseed he mentions the well-known patience associated with him and says also that mustardseed has caused his eyes to water (referring to the spice). To all the elves he has said that he looks forward to knowing them better.

COMMENT: *Titania's speech adds to our information about the fairy world that Shakespeare has created in this play. The activities described here paint an extraordinary scene of the whimsical, delightful, non-mortal world that Shakespeare has brought into being in this play. The list of foods – fruits and honey – is as beautiful as the many lists of flowers we have had before. We should note that moonbeams cannot be excluded from the scene.*

Bottom's easy graciousness with his extraordinary new companions is a mark of his marvellous ability to adapt immediately to whatever life offers him. His energetic love of life, his naïveté and eager innocence obtain his entrance into this other-world so different from his own. And he enjoys it to the fullest.

Titania now closes the scene by telling her elves to lead Bottom to her bower. She says the moon looks watery and when this happens the flowers weep, lamenting "some enforced chastity" (violated chastity). Bring him quietly, she orders, and they all leave.

COMMENT: *Titania's last words strike once again the keynote in this play's special atmosphere. She mentions:*

1. *the moon*
2. *flowers*
3. *love problems*

Notes

This scene accomplishes the following major things:

1.   The manner in which the Athenian workmen treat their play amplifies the relationship between illusion and reality – a theme at the heart of the play as a whole. These men are very certain which is which and they impose this attitude on their performance of "Pyramus and Thisbe." The result is comic in itself and is also in marked contrast to the confusions on this subject everywhere else in the play.

2.   Puck enters this world of simple realism and creates havoc by placing the head of an ass on Bottom. They have just been at great pains to show the man behind the lion's costume in their play and then Puck steps in and their very own bully Bottom is entirely changed into an ass from the neck

up with no man showing to reassure them at all. If such can happen in their solidly real world, then there are no limits possible to be fixed for sure between illusion and reality.

3.   The fantastically transformed Bottom, the last likely candidate for the role in the world before his transformation, now becomes a participator in the fairy world in the incredible position of being Titania's beloved. But we see that it was possible after all. He conducts himself with such sobriety and yet such grace, with his own good sense and yet with such enjoyment that we see that Bottom the weaver is supremely capable of uniting these disparate worlds. His love of life enables him to engage in it to the fullest. The fullness of his engagement unites experience. The union of reality and illusion empower him and are embodied in him.

ACT III · SCENE 2

This scene takes place in another part of the same wood. Oberon enters and wonders out loud what it was that Titania fell in love with under the charm he put on her. Puck enters and Oberon asks him what "night-rule" prevails in this "haunted grove." Puck launches right into a description of what he has done to Bottom and the other workmen and how Titania now loves a "monster." He says that near her bower where she lay asleep "a crew of patches, rude mechanicals" came to rehearse a play for Theseus' wedding celebration. Puck describes Bottom as "the shallowest thickskin of that barren sort" and tells Oberon how, when the workman went behind a hedge, he put an ass's head on him. He describes the havoc this caused among the other workmen when they saw their companion, in terms drawn from hunting – they scattered like wild geese or choughs at a gun shot. Puck continues in his characteristically graphic, rough and homey style to paint the disorder he created with his prank. And finally, says he, the "translated" Pyramus (Bottom), thus deserted by his terrified companions, is seen by the enchanted Titania: "Titania waked and straightway loved an ass."

Oberon says he is more than pleased with this result. He goes on to ask if Puck put the love-juice on the Athenian (meaning Demetrius). Puck says yes to this, and that the woman was nearby so he woke in love with her as Oberon intended (but Puck really enchanted Lysander by mistake). At this point, Hermia and Demetrius enter. Oberon says that here is the Athenian he spoke of. Puck, of course, says that this is the woman, but not the man. Then his mistake becomes evident, for of course these two discuss their situation. Demetrius left Helena before she awakened Lysander and was beloved of him by the power of the juice, so he knows nothing of that event. Lysander left Hermia sleeping when he set off to follow Helena, so Hermia is also completely in the dark on that score. All Demetrius knows is that Helena told him of the planned elopement and he wants Hermia for himself and has been searching for her. Now he has found her and he protests his great love for her as usual. She, of course, wants to know what has happened to her true love, Lysander, who had been sleeping by her side. He would *never* leave her and

51

she accuses Demetrius of killing him. Lysander was as true to her as the sun to the day, she says, and she would as soon believe that the moon could go through the center of the earth and shine in the daytime on the other side, as believe that Lysander would thus leave her. Demetrius must have murdered him. Demetrius still plays his love game, saying he's the one who's murdered by Hermia's cruelty to him.

Yet she's as beautiful as "yonder Venus in her glimmering sphere," even though she's a murderer. Poor Hermia has no patience with Demetrius's love prattle now. She wants her Lysander, and begs Demetrius for him. Demetrius replies that he would sooner give Lysander's carcass to his hounds than give him to Hermia. She can't stand this and reviles him thoroughly, begging him to speak the truth for once, and not be a double-tongued serpent, killer of a sleeping man. At this passionate outburst, Demetrius ceases his sweettalk and avows he neither killed him nor has any reason to think he is dead. Hermia begs him to reassure her. At her soft plea, Demetrius's designs on her reassert themselves and he callously asks what his reward will be for doing what she asks. Hermia's anger returns at his suggestive, leering remark and she says his reward is to never see her again. No matter how worried she is about Lysander, she'll stand no more of Demetrius's unpleasantness. She leaves and Demetrius remarks that it will do no good to plead his suit while she's in this temper, so he'll sleep there for awhile. Before doing so, he says a few pretty words on the subject. He then lies down and sleeps.

COMMENT: *We should note the gusto and vigor of Puck's inimitable style. He really enjoys recounting his mischief to his master, Oberon, and his vivid description of the poor "mechanicals" is one of the poetic high points of the play. We should also note that both Hermia and Demetrius cannot keep from mentioning the moon – the influence of this body is too pervasive ever to be absent. The way each uses it is very different, however. An indication that in this play the moon lends itself appropriately to any and every occasion. When Demetrius really angers her, Hermia's language becomes truly passionate and expressive of great feeling.*

Demetrius now lies asleep, and Oberon has been made fully aware of Puck's mistake. He says as much to him – Puck has turned a true love into a false one and has not turned any false love true. Puck says it's the rule of fate that for every man who keeps his oath, a million break them. Oberon instructs him to go swiftly through the wood and find Helena of Athens, whom he describes as pale and love-lorn. Bring her by some illusion, says Oberon, and meanwhile Demetrius will be charmed with the love juice in preparation for her appearance so that he will wake and love her. Puck sings that his departure is swifter that an arrow from a Tartar's bow, and he is off on his errand. Oberon then chants the charm over the sleeping Demetrius: the flower that was hit by Cupid's archery shall cause Demetrius to see Helena shining as gloriously as Venus in the sky. Puck re-enters and tells Oberon that Helena is close by. She is accompanied by Lysander, whom he mistook for Demetrius, and the spectacle they present is well worth watching, the mischievous spirit tells his master. "Lord, what fools these mortals be!" is Puck's famous reaction to the sight of Lysander pleading for Helena's love. Oberon says they must get out of the way, for the sound of Lysander's and Helena's voices will awaken Demetrius. Puck is delighted at the prospect of both men loving Helena at once. He loves preposterous things best, and this will really be something.

Lysander and Helena now enter. He is protesting the truth of his love vows, saying his tears prove that he is not wooing in scorn. Helena insists he's just being cunning. His vows belong to Hermia, and when he makes them to Helena they cancel each other out – his vows amount to nothing. Lysander says he had no judgment when he vowed his love to Hermia. Helena wisely observes that he has none now when he gives Hermia up. Lysander's next argument is that Demetrius loves Hermia and does not love Helena. At this crucial moment Demetrius wakes and immediately declares his great love for Helena in the most extravagant language. He calls her goddess, nymph, perfect, divine; he says her eyes are clearer than crystal, her lips more red than cherries, her hand more white than high mountain snow. Helena is understandably confounded by this declaration. In fact, she's outraged. "O spite! O hell!" she exclaims. She's of the confirmed opinion that they have joined together to make fun of her. She had earlier thought Lysander alone was making fun of her when he declared his undying devotion – now she suspects a league against her. She says, can't they merely hate her without so abusing her? It is not manly of them to carry on so as if they loved her when she knows they hate her. They are really rivals for Hermia's love and now they're just trying to outdo each other in mocking Helena. How low of them to make her cry with their derision, she says. No noble person would so torment and offend a young maid just to have the fun of it.

Lysander now takes it upon himself to reprimand Demetrius, saying that since he loves Hermia, Lysander will give over his claim to that girl. In exchange he'll take Helena, whom he now loves till his death. Helena here interjects her opinion of this as idle mockery and a waste of breath. Now Demetrius has his say, which is, of course, that Lysander can keep his Hermia. He only liked her temporarily, and now his affection has returned home to Helena for good. Lysander tells Helena not to believe Demetrius. Demetrius warns him to keep his opinion to himself, and points out to Lysander that his beloved Hermia is approaching. At this point Hermia, who knows nothing of all the latest goings on, enters. All she knows is that her Lysander disappeared from her side while she was asleep.

COMMENT: *Before the confusion in this foursome reaches its peak by the addition of the fourth member, let us note some points about the preceding developments. Puck's observation, that the proportion of constant men to inconstant men is one to a million, recalls the many earlier statements of man's inconstancy. Remember that Hermia swore to meet Lysander "by all the vows that ever men have broke," which is many more than women have ever made. And both Oberon and Theseus have a long history of amours. Even* *though the confusion is immediately caused by Puck's mistake, his opinion is that men in love are ridiculous anyway: "Lord, what fools these mortals be!"*

Archery (Tartar's bow; Cupid's archery) and the moon (Venus in the sky) should be noted as recurrent here. Lysander's claim to judgment in loving Helena now, as opposed to having had none when he loved Hermia before, reminds us again of this issue (the relationship between judgment and love). Demetrius wakes up exactly on cue, as Lysander is telling Helena that her beloved Demetrius doesn't love her, so why shouldn't she take Lysander as a substitute. And of course, enchanted as he is, Demetrius immediately spouts the most absurdly extravagant love-vows the minute he opens his eyes. He is utterly ridiculous. The first part of her that he chooses to praise is, ironically, her eyes. It is to be noted that Helena's reactions are very feelingly expressed and she becomes much more real to us as a character. In contrast to this, the two men still speak their customary wooden language, full of formal twists and turns on words – the same shallow tripe. Lysander wants to just swap girls with Demetrius – it's as simple as that, he says. Lysander's last words to Hermia were that he would love her till his death. Now he turns right around and says the same about Helena. The enchanted Demetrius is equally ridiculous: now, says he, I really know what I'm doing, so I've come back to Helena. In short, what we have here is the exact reverse of the initial situation when both men loved Hermia. At this point, both Lysander and Demetrius are madly in love with Helena, and nobody loves Hermia. The women haven't budged an inch – each loves her own man as always.

Now Hermia, who has been searching for her beloved Lysander, enters. All she knows is that she woke from a bad dream and found him gone. She has seen Demetrius since, but he was no help. He just annoyed her with his usual persistent wooing. When she finds out what's going on, the confusion will reach its hilarious peak. Hermia begins very sedately by observing that in the darkness her eyes didn't help her find Lysander, but her ears were more acute. She concludes by inquiring in a nice way as to why he left her. Since the confusion hasn't touched her yet, she speaks the usual lover-language of nicely turned, somewhat formal phrases. But she won't be left because love made him leave. Hermia asks what love could possibly make him leave her? Lysander says his love for Helena, who illumines the night more than do the moon and stars above. He asks Hermia why she followed him – didn't she realize that he left her because he hates her? Hermia can only say that Lysander cannot be speaking his real thoughts.

Helena, having heard this exchange between Lysander and Hermia, now thinks she sees what's going on: Hermia is in on the conspiracy against her. Consequently, Helena begins to reprimand Hermia for joining with Lysander and Demetrius in this "foul derision." Helena recounts all the girlhood pleasures and confidences she and Hermia have shared. She speaks of their sitting in the woods together, embroidering flowers, almost as if they were one person, so intimate was their friendship. She accuses Hermia of breaking these long-standing ties, and says she does an injury to the entire female sex in betraying her girlfriend and joining with men against her. Hermia is amazed at this outburst from Helena. To Hermia it seems that Helena scorns her, not vice versa. Helena explains more fully how things look to her. She thinks that Hermia has told Lysander to pretend that he loves Helena, and she has made her other love, Demetrius, do likewise. Why else should Demetrius, who has reviled Helena up till now, suddenly start praising and loving her? And what possible reason is there for Lysander to deny his love to Hermia except at Hermia's own instigation? Helena concludes with the self-pitying observation that since Hermia is so fortunate in love she ought to pity Helena who isn't, not despise her.

Hermia still can only say she doesn't understand what Helena means. Helena is more than ever convinced that Hermia merely pretends innocence, and she accuses them all once again of making fun of her. She says they all lack pity, grace and manners, and she'll just go away to her death somewhere. Lysander begs Helena to stay, calling her his life, his soul, his love. Helena ironically compliments his acting ability, and Hermia asks him not to scorn Helena thus. Demetrius adds his voice, saying he'll force Lysander to stop. Lysander says neither Hermia's entreaties nor Demetrius's threats can keep him from loving Helena more than life itself, and he'll lose his life to prove it. Demetrius says he loves Helena more, and he and Lysander move to fight for the proof. Hermia still asks what Lysander means by all this, and he answers, "Away, you Ethiope!" Demetrius taunts Lysander to follow and fight. Lysander shakes the clinging, loving Hermia off, and calls her a cat, a burr and a serpent. Hermia asks, "What change is this, Sweet love?" Lysander denies her: "Thy love? Out tawny Tartar, out!/Out, loathed med'cine! O hated potion, hence!" The astounded Hermia still can't believe her ears, and she inquires if Lysander is joking. Hearing this, Helena says that he is indeed joking and so is Hermia. Lysander reaffirms the challenge to fight with Demetrius, who replies that he doesn't trust Lysander, since he can't even shake Hermia off to get away for the fight. Lysander answers that even though he hates Hermia, he won't harm her. To this callous distinction, Hermia replies meaningfully. She finally begins to see that Lysander means what he says, and she observes that he can do her no greater harm than to hate her.

The word finally sinks in and she repeats it: "Hate me? Wherefore? O me, what news, my love?/Am not I Hermia? Are you not Lysander?" She points out the obvious fact that she is as fair as ever, that just last night he loved her, and the same night he left her. Heaven forbid that he left her in earnest, Hermia concludes. Lysander says absolutely and positively yes to this question, and swears on his life as well. He says he never wanted to see her again when he left. He mercilessly pounds home the fact that he loves Helena and hates Hermia – beyond a doubt, a hope, a question, for certain, nothing truer, and no joke. At this most fierce and cruel denunciation from Lysander, Hermia turns on Helena. She calls her friend a juggler, a canker blossom, and a thief of love, who came by night and stole her Lysander's heart from her. Helena pretends to compliment Hermia on her acting ability, chides her for her brazen behavior in joking along with the men, accuses her of trying to get a rise out of Helena by pretending thus, and finally Helena calls Hermia a "counterfeit" and a "puppet." When she hears the word "puppet," Hermia thinks she begins to understand what's going on. The shorter Hermia says she now sees that Helena has won Lysander by comparing their heights, and her being taller has won him. She says Helena has grown so high in Lysander's esteem because Hermia is "so dwarfish and so low." Hermia calls Helena a "painted maypole," and says she's not too "low" to reach Helena's eyes with her nails. Helena is afraid of Hermia now, and pleads with the men to protect her, for she is very cowardly and no match for Hermia even though she is taller than Hermia.

Hermia notes this last reference to her lack of height. Helena now pleads with Hermia not to be so bitter, saying she always loved Hermia. But she adds the confession that she told Demetrius of the planned elopement in order to have his thanks and his company. Helena explains how Demetrius mistreated her in the wood, and now all she wants is to go back to Athens without any fuss, taking her foolishness with her. Hermia says that she should just leave then, who's stopping her. Helena replies that she leaves a foolish heart behind. Hermia asks if she leaves it with Lysander. Helena says she leaves it with Demetrius. Lysander tells Helena not to be afraid of Hermia, and Demetrius jumps in to be her protector too. Helena now says how fierce Hermia is when she is angry, and that she was a "vixen" at school despite her small size. Hermia is very annoyed at this repeated reference to her short stature and attempts to get to Helena. Lysander takes it upon himself to revile Hermia in particularly this way now, calling her "dwarf," "minimus," "bead," "acorn." Demetrius says Lysander meddles too much with Helena, who scorns him. Demetrius says Lysander will be sorry if he insists on demonstrating his love for Helena. Lysander says now he's free of Hermia, and he'll fight with Demetrius to see who gets Helena. Demetrius is eager to do so, and the men leave. Hermia addresses Helena now and says this whole mess is because of her. Helena backs off, saying she won't trust Hermia, nor remain in her quarrelsome company. Hermia's hands are quicker to fight, says Helena, but Helena's legs, being longer, are good for running away. Hermia can only reply, "I am amazed, and know not what to say," and both girls leave.

COMMENT: *We have seen now the full result of Puck's mischief. The girls, who have remained constant to their original loves, bear the brunt of the confusion. Helena firmly believes the other three have joined together to make fun of her. Hermia comes to believe that Helena has won Lysander by being taller than Hermia. From their quarrel, we learn that Helena was played by a tall, light actor, and Hermia by a small, dark person. Note that at first Helena speaks of the idyllic friendship she shared with Hermia. After Hermia frightens Helena, however, the latter changes her tune: (1) She speaks of how Hermia was a vixen at school, and given to fierce outbursts. (2) Instead of just recalling their mutual trust, she now admits to having betrayed her friend's elopement to Demetrius. Hermia, from being beloved by two, is now completely unloved and unwanted. Her accusation that Helena has used her* *greater height to win Lysander is the foolish frenzy she is plunged into by the incomprehensible behavior of her companions. Her utter confusion is best expressed by her calling their very identities into question: "Am I not Hermia? Are you not Lysander?" she queries piteously. We cannot help but feel sorry for these tormented girls. Under the extreme pressure of these developments, the style in which the lovers speak becomes much more exciting and vivid. The men never lose their ridiculous habits – Lysander keeps swearing on his life, first one way, then the other; Demetrius is still the quintessential braggart, pompous and self-important. But note that Lysander is much more convincing in expressing his hate, much more truly passionate and feeling than when he was reciting his love to Hermia.*

With all four lovers gone, Oberon addresses Puck, and lays the above havoc at his doorstep. It is Puck's negligence that is the cause, and he either made a mistake once again, or else did the mischief on purpose. Puck vows that he made a mistake. After all, he did apply the juice to someone wearing Athenian clothes as Oberon commanded. However, he freely admits that he takes great pleasure in the way things turned out – their "jangling" is a real spectator sport to him. Oberon now says that since the two men have gone off to fight, he wants Robin to make the night foggy and lead the rivals astray so they don't ever come at each other. The King tells him to imitate each man's voice, alternately stirring them up and leading them on, but always in opposite directions. Keep them thus separated till they grow very sleepy. Then, says Oberon, crush another juice on the sleeping Lysander's eyes. This second juice has the effect of removing the enchantment from his eyes so that he will love Hermia as before. Thus, Oberon continues, they will all four wake up and think all that has passed is only a "dream and fruitless vision." They will go back to Athens, correctly paired two-by-two, and remain so till death. Oberon concludes by saying that in the meantime he'll go to Titania and get the little Indian boy. Once he has this object of his desire, he'll release the Queen from the love charm, she'll no longer love the monster, and everything will be peaceful. Puck says all this must be done quickly because the dawn is approaching. He speaks of how ghosts and damned spirits who have been wandering all night must now return to their unquiet graves at crossroads or under water. They are too ashamed to have the light of day shine on them, and they willfully deny themselves daylight and only go out at night. Oberon, says, "But we are spirits of another sort." And he very beautifully describes how he has enjoyed the morning. He may stay abroad in full daylight while the red sun turns the green sea into gold. But, he concludes, let us still be quick with our business, and we'll get it done before daybreak.

COMMENT: *Oberon here tells us how he will make everything all right. It will take time to do it, and this will be the business of the remainder of the play. Fortunately, and expectedly, the King of Fairies happens to have another juice which acts as an antidote to the first one from "the little western flower." Puck will apply this latter cure to Lysander, while Oberon himself will do the same to Titania after he has obtained the little Indian boy. We now* *are reminded that all this has come about because Oberon wants a changeling whom Titania has excellent reasons for wishing to keep for herself (the mother of the little boy was a dear friend who died in childbirth). Thus, despite his beautiful poetry and his kingly power, when we remember this original fact, Oberon comes off little better than the two male lovers. For magnanimity of spirit and depth of emotion, he's about on a par with them.*

Puck's speech about damned spirits tells us what the spirits in this play are not like, for Oberon denies any kinship. The speech of the King in which he does this is another example of the supreme beauty that Shakespeare has given to Oberon's poetic utterances. Coming after the frenzied "jangling" (Puck's most appropriate word) of the lovers, Oberon's poetry affords us a refreshing resting-place. We lose our misgivings about his share in causing all this trouble, or rather it seems unimportant when bathed in the golden light of his poetry. After the obfuscation of the night we have been in we can only revel joyously in the morning he creates with his words.

After Oberon speaks of his delight in the morning, he leaves to find Titania. Puck remains to do his job on Lysander and Demetrius. He chants a song in happy anticipation of how he will mislead them. Then he spies Lysander, who enters searching for Demetrius. Puck speaks in Demetrius's voice and Lysander exits again in an attempt to follow the voice he has heard. Now Demetrius enters, having heard Lysander answer Puck, and demands that Lysander to Demetrius and eggs him on. Demetrius cannot find his foe and now Puck says he should follow his voice and leads him away. Lysander re-enters when they have gone and complains that as fast as he follows, Demetrius runs away even faster. He says he'll rest till daylight comes to help him find Demetrius, and he lies down and sleeps. Now Puck and Demetrius come back, and Puck is still leading Demetrius on. Demetrius dares him to wait and face up to the fight, and says he just runs away. Puck continues to imitate Lysander, till finally Demetrius is exasperated with the fruitless pursuit and he too says he'll catch his foe in daylight. Then he lies down and sleeps. Now Helena enters, complaining of her weariness, and desiring daylight to come to show her the way back to Athens so she may escape the company of these that hate her. She bids sleep come to put her out of her sorrowful condition for a time. Then she goes to sleep also. Now Puck comments that one more is needed to make up the complete company – two of each kind, he says. He comments, "Cupid is a knavish lad/Thus to make poor females mad." Now Hermia enters, weary and woebegone. She can go no further, she says, and will rest where she is till daylight. Her last words before sleeping ask that the heavens protect her Lysander if there is a fight between him and Demetrius.

Now Puck chants over Lysander and applies the curative to Lysander's eyelids. Puck's song says that when Lysander wakes he will take "True delight/In the sight/Of thy former lady's eye." Puck concludes his song and the scene with a country proverb: Every man should take his own. When every

Jack has his Jill all will be well, predicts Puck, and with his pronouncement on life the scene closes.

Notes

In this long and eventful scene, the following takes place:

1.   Puck tells Oberon how he transformed Bottom, and how Titania fell in love with him.

2.   Puck's mistaken application of the love-charm to Lysander instead of to Demetrius becomes known when Hermia is seen begging Demetrius for information on Lysander's whereabouts.

3.   To remedy the situation, Oberon enchants Demetrius and sends Puck to find Helena so that Demetrius may fall in love with her.

4.   This makes matters even worse, because now both men love Helena at once, and there is frantic quarreling and confusion when all four lovers get together.

5.   Finally, Lysander is disenchanted so that he will love Hermia again. Oberon goes to take the charm off Titania. The lovers are left sleeping and when they awake everything will be all right. They will think it was only a dream, says Oberon.

CONTRASTS IN LOVERS   Shakespeare, for the love of fun, and in harmony with the spirit of the play, brings together lovers of different temperament. Demetrius, sharp-tongued, aggressive, and ready with his sword, is made to fall in love with the modest, weeping, timorous Helena, while Lysander, slow to anger, tearful, and poetic, takes Hermia, the vixen, sarcastic, passionate, and ready with her finger nails. However, when the occasion arises, he too is rich in insulting repartee and quickness of self-defense.

GHOSTS   Oberon's explanation of ghosts has nothing to do with the action or progress of the play. It is included to make clear to an ignorant and wondering audience the difference between fairies and ghosts and to explain why the former may still be encountered in daytime.

DRAMATIC PAUSE   Line 49 contains only four syllables instead of the usual ten. As used here it contributes what is called a dramatic pause, implying that the actor is to pause before continuing with the following line. Hermia's request to Lysander to kill her is dramatic and she pauses to let its full significance be borne in upon him. Possibly she has grown breathless in her passionate outbreak and pauses to regain control of herself.

ACT IV · SCENE 1

We now return to the situation we left at the end of Act III, Scene 1, where Titania is madly in love with the transformed Bottom. This scene opens with the entrance of Titania, Bottom, and the attendant fairies. Oberon is behind them. Titania is speaking lovingly to Bottom. She wants him to sit down so she can stroke his cheeks, crown him with musk-roses, and kiss his "fair large ears." Bottom, completely at home in his new environment, calls for Peaseblossom. He asks the latter to scratch his head, and then call "Monsieur Cobweb" to him and tell him to bring him some honey, adding considerately that the fairy ought to be careful not to drown in it. Bottom asks "Monsieur Mustardseed" to help "Cavalery Cobweb" scratch Bottom's head. Bottom remarks that he must go to the barber's soon, for he has an extraordinary amount of hair on his face, and he is "such a tender ass" that it tickles him. Titania asks her beloved if he would like some music, and he answers that he would like the "tongs and the bones." The Queen also inquires what he might like to eat, and Bottom replies that he wants provender, oats, and hay. Titania suggests nuts, but Bottom would rather have dried peas. What he most desires right at the moment, however, is to sleep. Titania dismisses all the fairies and, holding Bottom in her arms as the woodbine twists around the honeysuckle or as the ivy encircles the elm, they both sleep.

Puck enters and Oberon advances to meet him, pointing out the sight of Titania and Bottom together. Oberon says he is beginning to pity Titania's condition. He met her while she was waiting upon Bottom and he taunted her for it. She begged his patience and he then requested the changeling, which she gave him immediately. Oberon adds the detail that the flowers with which she had crowned Bottom had dew standing in them like tears at the disgrace of being used for such a purpose. Now that Oberon has the boy, he tells Puck, he will take the charm off his Queen's eyes. He instructs Puck to remove the ass's head from Bottom so that the latter may return to Athens with everyone else. Oberon says that Bottom will think his experience to be no more than "the fierce vexation of a dream." Before Puck restores Bottom, Oberon will release Titania. Oberon recites a chant over her that says she will see with her customary eyes, and that "Dian's bud" will overpower "Cupid's flower."

Then he wakes her, and Titania says, "My Oberon, what visions have I seen!/Methought I was enamored of an ass." Oberon points to Bottom and says she loved him. Titania wants to know how that came to be, saying she hates his sight now. Oberon asks her to be silent for awhile, he tells Puck to remove the ass's head from Bottom, and he tells Titania to call for music that will put Bottom into a deep sleep. Titania and Puck do what Oberon has bid, music plays, and the King and Queen dance hand in hand. Oberon says that he and his Queen, in renewed harmony, will dance in Theseus' house the next night and bless it. The two pairs of lovers will also be wedded in all happiness. Puck calls Oberon's attention to the sound of the morning lark. Oberon says they will leave then, adding that they can circle the world "swifter than the wand'ring moon." Titania asks that on their flight she be told how she happened to be sleeping on the ground with all the mortals. All the fairies leave.

COMMENT: *Bottom conducts himself with propriety at the court of the Fairy Queen. The French mode of address was proper courtly behavior. His "Cavalery" is his own version of Cavalier, which is a title of address for a gallant. He is at his ease and enjoying himself. His remarks about the hair on his face are funny because he doesn't know he has an ass's head, and when he* *calls himself "a tender ass" he is unknowingly even funnier. The food he requests is appropriate to an ass – hay, oats, provender, dried peas. The music that he requests, though he claims to have a good ear, is not very tuneful. This is still fairyland, so flowers are mentioned: musk-roses, woodbine, honeysuckle, and ivy. Titania applies the words "amiable" and "gentle" to Bottom while she is enchanted, but in truth his behavior here warrants this praise. Though she is not herself when she says this of Bottom, Titania's description is accurate. We laugh at Bottom, but we like him too. Flowers and the moon figure in Oberon's speeches above also. Music pervades this fairy world and is part of the magic that prevails. Oberon says that Bottom will think that he has had a dream; when Titania awakens she refers to the visions that she has seen. The events of the night are thus going to pass for mere illusion with some of those who have experienced them. But Oberon can point out the real, undeniable evidence to Titania in the shape of the transformed Bottom. This should be kept in mind when the others wake up and question the reality of their experience.*

Heralded by the sound of a horn, Theseus and all his attendants enter, accompanied by Hippolyta and Egeus. Theseus speaks, saying that now their performance of the May morning ritual is over and while it's still early he'll exhibit his fine hunting hounds to Hippolyta. He commands that the dogs be let loose so that she may hear the music of their barking, and he sends for the forester. The forester is the manager of game and hunting preparations in the royal forest. Theseus tells Hippolyta that they'll go up to the mountain-top to listen to the interplay of barking with echoes. She says she was with Hercules and Cadmus in Crete when they hunted a bear with Spartan hounds. She said she never heard such beautiful sounds – groves, skies, fountains, every place was filled with a concert of sound. "I never heard/So musical a discord, such sweet thunder," Hippolyta says. Theseus is moved by this praise to claim more for his own hounds. The Duke waxes poetic in this famous description. His dogs are of the Spartan breed, and they have the same dewlaps, sandy color, long ears, and thick legs. Though slow, they are "matched in mouth like bells,/Each under each." Theseus' enthusiasm for this latter quality leads him to say that more harmonious sounds never accompanied hunting anywhere, be it Crete, Sparta, or Thessaly, and he tells Hippolyta to decide when she hears. At this moment, Theseus notices the four lovers asleep on the ground, and inquires who they are. Egeus names his daughter Hermia, Lysander, Demetrius, and Nedar's daughter Helena, and he says he wonders what they're all doing there. Theseus says they probably got up early to celebrate May Day and came to the wood because they heard the Duke was celebrating the day in the wood. Theseus asks Egeus if this is the day that Hermia is supposed to announce her choice between Demetrius as a husband on the one hand, and death or a nunnery on the other. Egeus says that it is, and Theseus orders that the huntsman wake the sleeping lovers by blowing the hunting horns. This is done, and they all start up.

Theseus greets them and makes a joke about St. Valentine's Day, when, it was thought, birds began to mate. Lysander asks the Duke's pardon. Theseus requests that they stand up, and he says he knows that the two men are rivals, so how is it that they are here together asleep? Lysander says he can only reply in amazement himself and still half-asleep, but, though he hesitates to say for certain, he thinks he came into the woods with Hermia. Yes, that was it – he came to the woods with Hermia in order to flee the Athenian law. Egeus doesn't let him get any further with his explanation. The enraged father demands the law on Lysander's head, and points out to Demetrius how Lysander was trying to cheat him. Demetrius now speaks and says Helena told him of the planned elopement. He followed them in fury, and she followed him in fancy. But, continues Demetrius, though he's at a loss to say *which* power, some power for sure has dissolved completely his love for Hermia, which now seems just the memory of a childhood toy. Furthermore, he is now completely enamoured of Helena, his heart belongs to Helena, he can see only Helena. Demetrius explains that he was betrothed to Helena before he loved Hermia, and he must have been like a sick man whose appetite is malfunctioning to have ever stopped loving her. Now, he's like a man returned to a healthy state who has his natural appetite again, and he loves Helena and will continue to forever. Theseus says to the lovers that their meeting was fortunate, and he'll hear more of their story later. The Duke tells Egeus that he overrides the father's wishes with respect to his daughter, and the two couples shall be married when he and Hippolyta are. Since the day has grown later, there won't be any hunting and they'll all go back to Athens for a stately feast. Theseus bids Hippolyta come and they leave with Egeus.

COMMENT: *Hippolyta's reminiscence of a hunting with Hercules and Cadmus is not in any of the legends about Hippolyta. However, in some accounts, Theseus was a companion of Hercules in his Amazonian exploits, and hunted the Caledonian boar with other heroes. Hounds of Sparta and of Crete were celebrated breeds in antiquity. Despite the allusions to antiquity, the whole passage is made up of English hunting terminology. We should notice the contrast between this music, so highly praised by Theseus and Hippolyta, and the music that permeated the fairy world, to which Oberon and Titania just danced and sang before their departure a few lines before the entrance of the royal party. Of course, the coincidence of the lovers' being found by the royal party just after the fairies left them is what we have been accustomed to expect in this play. Note that the dew which bedecked flowers in the fairy world is now brushed by the long ears of bull-like hounds. Theseus is reigning in his world.*

Lysander and Demetrius are vaguely aware of strange happenings and powers, but they don't know for sure. In any event, they are finally matched to the right girl friends, just as Oberon predicted. Of course, Demetrius is still under the effect of the love juice. We must keep this in mind when he describes how he's like a sick man returned to health now that he loves Helena again. And our awareness of this fact colors our attitude toward his proclamation of undying, permanent, perfect love for Helena. He's really still enchanted.

After Theseus, Hippolyta, and Egeus have left, the lovers remain behind for a few moments to exchange expressions of amazement at their condition. Demetrius says things seem like mountains seen at such a great distance that they look like clouds. Hermia says it's like seeing double. Helena agrees with her, and says she can't believe she really has her Demetrius – it's like finding a jewel by accident. Demetrius asks the others if they're sure they're all awake. It seems to him that he's still asleep and dreaming. He asks if the Duke came and bid them leave with him. Hermia says yes, and her father, too. Helena adds Hippolyta, and Lysander contributes that they were indeed bid to go with Theseus to the temple. Demetrius says that they must be awake then, and they ought to follow the Duke and tell each other their dreams on the way. The lovers leave.

COMMENT: *We should note that the lovers express their confusion in terms of eyesight. Helena is accurate when she speaks of feeling as though finding Demetrius is like finding a jewel by sheer accident. She says, "Mine own, and not mine own." And we know Demetrius is still under the power of Oberon's charm. Note that Demetrius has the most to say here and he speaks of their night's experiences as "a dream."*

After the lovers have left, Bottom wakes up. He thinks he's still rehearsing "Pyramus and Thisbe." His first words are that he should be summoned when his cue comes, and he gives his next cue, "Most fair Pyramus." Suddenly he wakes up enough to realize he's alone, and he calls for his companions, Quince, Flute, Snout, and Starveling. He says that they've stolen away and left him asleep, and what a "most rare vision" he's had meanwhile. Bottom's famous reaction to his experience is, "I've had a dream, past the wit of man to say what dream it was. Man is but an ass if he go about to expound this dream." Bottom begins to say what happened to him, but he breaks off and says only a fool would attempt to say what happened to him. None of man's senses can apprehend his dream, he says. In describing this, he confuses all the senses and applies them to the wrong bodily organ: the eye can't hear, the ear can't see, the hand can't taste, the tongue can't conceive, and the heart can't report what his dream was. He says he'll get Peter Quince to write a ballad on his dream. It will be called "Bottom's Dream" because it has no bottom, he says. He will sing it at the end of their play before the Duke, perhaps at Thisbe's death. Bottom's departure here ends the scene.

COMMENT: *Bottom himself has told us that the profundity of his "dream" defies any comment. And indeed, his own manner of reacting to it is the best approach to the experience. Wonder, awe, and a strong sense of the power beyond man's apprehension are communicated by his words here. The confusions he commits in assigning the senses to the wrong organs are perfectly in keeping with the dramatic opposition of reality and illusion at the heart of this play. The name "Bottom's Dream" is, as he realizes, correct in both the ways he says. It is his dream, but the profundity of its implications are beyond him and he feels this power.*

Notes

In this scene, the following takes place:

1.   Titania is disenchanted and awakened. She is going to be told immediately what happens, and she is shown the object of her past passion right in the flesh before her.

2.   The lovers were brought to rights at the end of the last scene, but they don't know it yet. After we have seen Titania back to normal, we now return to the sleeping lovers who are awakened by Theseus. Demetrius now loves Helena, and Lysander still loves Hermia. The Duke says they'll have a triple wedding together.

3.   Last to awaken is Bottom, who rightly declares the unfathomability of his "dream" and feels most profoundly its power.

ACT IV · SCENE 2

In this scene we are back in Athens with the workmen. Quince, Flute, Snout, and Starveling enter. Quince asks if anyone's been to Bottom's house to inquire if he's come home yet. Starveling says he hasn't been heard from yet, and that doubtless he's been "transported," meaning either carried off or transformed. Flute says that their play will be spoiled if he doesn't come back. They can't do it without him. Quince agrees with this, saying that no one in all Athens can play Pyramus except Bottom. Flute says Bottom has the best mind of any workman in Athens. Quince agrees and adds that Bottom has the best appearance and voice too. He uses the word "paramour" when he means "paragon" and Flute corrects him saying that a "paramour" is nothing. Snug enters with the news that the Duke has left the temple and that there are "two or three lords and ladies more married." If they had been able to perform their play it would have done them a lot of good. Flute bemoans Bottom's missing the pension the Duke surely would have granted him after seeing his marvelous performance as Pyramus. He would have deserved sixpence a day for sure. At this moment, Bottom enters, inquiring lovingly for his friends. He calls them "lads" and "hearts." Quince exclaims with joy and calls the day "courageous" and the hour "most happy." Bottom tells his friends that he'll tell them wonders, but they mustn't ask what. Then he says he'll tell them everything just as it happened. Quince asks to hear. Now Bottom won't say a word, except that the Duke is through dinner, and they must get ready to perform their play. He instructs them to be clean and well-groomed, except for the lion's long nails, and not to eat onions or garlic. Thus they'll have sweet breath and their play will be considered a sweet comedy. He bids them depart without further talk and they all leave.

COMMENT: *We should note that this scene, and Bottom's speech at the end of the last scene, are in prose. These characters always speak in prose. The conversation before Bottom arrives exhibits the great concern and affection Bottom's friends have for him. His first words to them show that this* *is mutual. Bottom seems to be about to tell his friends about the experience he has had, but for now anyway, he just can't. All immediate interest is turned toward the play to be presented before the Duke.*

Notes

The purpose of this short scene is to show Bottom's return to normal. Although the scene is very brief, we do learn some important things:

1.   Bottom is loved and admired by his friends and they are very sad at his strange disappearance. Their remarks convey warm and true feeling. They may not be gentlemen, but they are gentle, simple men with admirable qualities.

2.   Bottom returns to them warm and real as always. His first words are full of the special quality that is Bottom: "Where are these lads? where are these hearts?" Direct, energetic, and above all loving, he takes charge with his accustomed vigor and enthusiasm.

3.   Finally, we learn that their play of "Pyramus and Thisbe" has been selected as the evening's entertainment at court where several more people have been married. It really doesn't matter how many (Snug says two or three more couples), for as Flute points out, "a paramour is, God bless us, a thing of naught." From what we have seen in the moonlight of the mad wood, this point of view seems right enough.

ACT V · SCENE 1

In this scene we are back in Theseus' palace again. Theseus, Hippolyta, Philostrate, Lords, and Attendants enter. Hippolyta remarks that what the lovers have spoken of is strange. Theseus answers in a famous speech about the lover, the madman and the poet. He says the lovers' story is "more strange than true," and he for one never believes old stories and fairy tales. Lovers and madmen have "seething brains" that grasp more than reason can understand. In fact, he continues, the lunatic, the lover, and the poet all have the same kind of imagination, they just imagine different things. The madman sees more devils than there are in hell. The equally frantic lover imagines a mere gypsy to be as beautiful as Helen of Troy. The frenzied eye of the poet looks back and forth between heaven and earth and whatever the imagination comes up with, he with his pen gives a shape and a name to it. In Theseus' famous words, the poet "gives to airy nothing/A local habitation and a name." He says the imagination has such "tricks" that if it wants to grasp a joy, it can use reason to understand how to bring that joy. Theseus concludes with the example of being frightened at night and thinking that a bush is a bear.

However, Hippolyta still says that the whole story, with everyone's minds "transfigured so together," is more than fanciful imaginings. The story exhibits great constancy, even though it is strange and admirable. Theseus says that the lovers are coming, mirthful and joyous. At this point, Lysander, Demetrius, Hermia, and Helena enter, and Theseus wishes them joy and love. Lysander replies with the wish that the Duke have even more of the same. Theseus asks what entertainment is available to pass the time away between after-supper and bed-time. He calls for Philostrate, the manager of entertainment at court, and the latter says that he is here. Theseus asks him what entertainment is available and Philostrate hands him a list of possibilities which the Duke reads out loud. Out of four choices he selects "Pyramus and Thisbe" and questions Philostrate about it. The description given him interests him by its strange combinations: "A tedious brief scene of young Pyramus/And his love Thisbe; very tragical mirth" is what the tradesmen have called their offering. Theseus comments on the combination of opposites. Philostrate explains that though the play is very short indeed, it is tedious to watch because it is performed so badly; and though Pyramus kills himself, the whole performance made Philostrate laugh.

Theseus asks who the players are and is told about the efforts of the Athenian workmen who are rank amateurs completely unaccustomed to using their minds. Theseus says he wants to see the play. Philostrate tries to dissuade him, saying the only thing amusing about it is how hard they try. But Theseus insists on his choice, saying that if their intentions are good that's all that counts, and he sends Philostrate to get the performers. Hippolyta says she doesn't want to watch these workmen struggle and fail to please. Theseus says she needn't worry, and she replies that Philostrate said they were completely inept. Theseus says that, in that case, more kindness and nobility will be required of the audience. He tells her how he is often confronted with tongue-tied public officials and yet he knows that they mean well. Philostrate comes back and says that the Prologue of the play is ready to be spoken. Quince speaks his part and he doesn't punctuate and pause meaningfully, so it comes out all wrong. Theseus, Lysander, and Hippolyta remark how little sense his speech made. Each has a different metaphor for this. Next enter the rest of the actors: Pyramus, Thisbe, Wall, Moonshine, and Lion. Quince continues with the prologue and gives a summary of the story and introduces each character. They all leave except Wall. Theseus says he wonders if the lion will speak and Demetrius makes the joke that one lion may, since many asses do. Now Wall speaks and introduces himself as Snout, telling what his part is in the play. Through a chink in this wall the lovers whisper. Theseus and Demetrius remark on the wit of the wall in speaking so. Now Pyramus re-enters, and addresses the black night and the wall, asking where is his Thisbe. He looks through the chink and cannot see her. Theseus says the wall should answer, but Bottom tells him that's not the way the play goes. It is Thisbe's cue and she will enter in a moment, he patiently explains.

Thisbe enters and addresses her love-complaint to the wall that always separates her from Pyramus. Pyramus says that he "sees" her voice and he'll try to "hear" her face. The lovers then greet each other and liken their love to that of famous lovers in the past, only they make their usual errors in doing it. Instead of "Leander and Hero" they mention "Limander and Helen" and for "Cephalus" and "Procris" they say "Shafalus" and "Procrus." This loving exchange is in the form of single, alternating lines of dialogue, rhymed by twos ("stichomythia"). Pyramus and Thisbe arrange to meet at "Ninny's tomb" and Pyramus says he'll be there, come life or death. They exit, and so does Wall, after first saying that he's done his job so he's leaving. Theseus, Demetrius, and Hippolyta exchange comments on what they have just seen. They think it's silly and Theseus says all acting is just "shadows" requring the audience to use imagination. For this performance, one has to use a little more imagination, that's all. Lion and Moonshine re-enter now, and Lion explains that he's really Snug the joiner so the ladies won't be frightened. Theseus, Demetrius, and Lysander must comment here too, and they exchange supercilious witticisms about the discretion and valor of Lion. Now Moonshine tries to explain his characterization, but Demetrius and Theseus persist in their disruptive comments. Their joke is that old stand-by about horns, since Moonshine says he is the "horned" (crescent) moon. Hippolyta says she is weary of the moon and wishes it would change. Theseus makes another comment and finally Moonshine gets to speak his whole speech.

But as soon as he finishes, Demetrius must unnecessarily point out that all the objects that Starveling is carrying ought to be inside the lantern since they are inside the moon. Now Thisbe re-enters to keep her appointment at "Ninny's tomb" and she is frightened away by the roar of Lion. Demetrius, Theseus, and Hippolyta compliment Lion, Thisbe and Moon. Hippolyta had said she was weary of the moon, but here she says, "Truly, the moon shines with a good grace." The Lion now shakes the mantle Thisbe dropped before he exists. Theseus, Lysander and Demetrius comment briefly. Pyramus comes in now and, seeing the blood-stained mantle of Thisbe, recites a passionate speech. Theseus says it almost makes a man sad to see this. Hippolyta remarks feelingly, "Beshrew my heart, but I pity the man." Pyramus continues his passionate expression of grief and concludes by killing himself. Moonshine exits and Pyramus dies. Demetrius, Lysander, and Theseus comment once again. Hippolyta inquires how Thisbe will find her lover with the moon gone, and Theseus replies that she will find him by starlight. Thisbe re-enters and Hippolyta says that she hopes she'll be brief. Demetrius and Lysander also comment. Thisbe finds Pyramus and, after first thinking he's asleep, she sorrows deeply over his death. She describes him as having the colors of various flowers: "lily lips," "cherry nose," "yellow cowslip cheeks," and eyes "green as leeks." She calls on the Fates who have killed him to end her life, and she stabs herself to death. Theseus says that Moonshine and Lion are now left to bury the dead lovers. Demetrius adds Wall. At this, Bottom starts up and explains that the wall of hostility between their two families is now no longer. He asks if the audience wishes to see an epilogue or to hear a dance.

Theseus says no epilogue is needed and compliments them on the performance. He requests that they perform their dance instead. Afterwards, the Duke announces that it is midnight and time for bed. It's almost "fairy time" says Theseus and he's afraid they'll oversleep the next morning from being up so late. The performance of "Pyramus and Thisbe" has made the evening pass very quickly. He concludes by saying that they'll continue to celebrate for another fortnight (two weeks), and with these words, everyone leaves.

COMMENT: *Duke Theseus' speech about the lover, madman, and poet expresses the view of the practical, successful man of affairs. He does his public job very well, is a brave soldier and a trustworthy leader. However, the wondrous realms of art and love are to him as unapproachable as madness. Hippolyta is more open than he and she feels the power of these other realms.*

Having the performance of a play take place within the larger play as a whole allows Shakespeare to show us the reactions of those characters who witness it. That is the case here, and while Lysander and Demetrius are joking at the expense of the earnest tradesmen, we should remember how absurdly they behaved in the woods. Demetrius does most of the disruptive jesting, and it is he who still has the love juice on his eyes that causes him to love Helena. Notice that Helena and Hermia, who have been constant to their loves, do not engage in the jesting aimed at the workmen's performance.

When everyone has left, Puck enters. He describes the night – the wild animals that roar, howl, and screech; the ghosts that leave their graves to wander abroad; and the fairies like himself that "follow darkness like a dream," and at night make merry. He says nothing shall disturb Theseus' house, and he has been sent with a broom to sweep there. Oberon and Titania enter with their attendants, and the fairies sing and dance. Oberon bids his subjects go about the house blessing everyone. He himself will bless the royal union so that they shall love forever and have perfect offspring. He hands out "field-dew" to be sprinkled in blessing everywhere, and instructs everyone to meet at daybreak. The King and Queen leave with their followers. Puck has the last words in the play. He says that if the play has not pleased but offended, just write it off as a dream. If they're lucky enough to escape being hissed and booed, then he promises they'll improve. And if the audience applauds, then Puck will do good for them. With this, the spirit exits and the play ends.

COMMENT: *We have seen Snug play a lion, and when Puck enters he describes the real night inhabited by fierce animals and frightening sounds. He speaks of cleaning the palace because Puck is traditionally represented as having a broom and cleaning the houses of those whom he favored. Oberon speaks of preventing disfigured children because folklore ascribed this power to fairies. We should note that once again dew is mentioned. It is fitting that Puck should have the last word, and that he suggest to us the possibility of the whole play's being only a dream. This has been "A Midsummer Night's Dream."*

Notes

In the last scene of the play the following is accomplished:

1. All the lovers have been married to the right persons.

2. The workmen perform at court the play they have prepared for this purpose.

3.   The fairies enter when all else is done and bless all with peace and prosperity.

Thus, all strands are woven together harmoniously.

Character Sketches
Theseus

Shakespeare's Theseus is really a romantic rather than a classical character. As Duke of Athens he reminds us somewhat of Henry V, King of England. He appears to be Shakespeare's earlier conception of his ideal king. Like King Henry he is a great warrior and a ruler possessed of much dignity and majesty. He bears some resemblance to the English king also in the fact that his youth had been rather wild and dissolute (Act II, Sc. 1, 76-81). But that was when he was still under the influence of the fairies, an influence which passed away before the period of his life presented in the play. Here we see him as a soldier and a man of action, who wooed his wife with his sword, and 'won her love doing her injuries', and who in times of peace loved to hear the music of his hounds. His career has been one of conquest (Act V, Sc. 1, 51, 93-100), his triumphs have been celebrated in set orations prepared by great scholars who have 'shivered and looked pale' in the presence of so famous a soldier. But he, being a man of action rather than of words, who could appreciate any service done him 'when simpleness and duty tender it', has a preference for 'the modesty of fearful duty' rather than for

> The rattling tongue
> Of saucy and audacious eloquence
>
> (Act V, Sc. 1, 102)

His love for Hippolyta is no romantic passion like the loves of his young Athenian friends. Indeed, although he makes love at the beginning of the play in a dignified and stately fashion, we find him later comparing together 'the lunatic, the lover and the poet,' apparently without any idea of including himself in his description (Act V, Sc. 1, 7-20). He is certainly not unimaginative, but he keeps his imagination well under control and therein differs from those who 'are of imagination all compact'. He cannot believe in the visions and dreams of the lovers in the forest, in 'these antique fables, nor these fairy toys'. His life has been too full of action and hard work to allow him to let his imagination run riot, but he has a very true idea of 'the pleasures of the imagination'. Unlike Hippolyta, to whom the Interlude is simply 'the silliest stuff that ever I heard', he can find enjoyment in the honest attempts of imperfect actors. He can 'piece out their imperfections with his thoughts'. To him 'the best in this kind are but shadows and the worst are no worse if imagination amend them'.

Theseus is kind and generous and shows a strong inclination to make everyone happy in his kingdom. He proclaims a fortnight's holiday on the occasion of his marriage. He endeavours to persuade Hermia to submit to her father's will, and though, being himself a ruler, he naturally upholds the Athenian law, yet we feel all the time that his sympathies are with the daughter rather than with the stern parent. When Demetrius expresses his determination to be true to his first love, the Duke unhesitatingly overrides the will of Egeus. During the Interlude he apologises for the imperfections of the actors, takes in very good humour the amusing corrections of Bottom (Act V, Sc. 1, 184-7 and 354-5), and sends away the players delighted with the assurance that it is 'a fine tragedy, and very notably discharged'.

It would appear that Shakespeare was not concerned with depicting the character of Theseus as an Athenian monarch of a pagan age. Rather, he has really painted the picture of a contemporary English hunting squire. His pleasure is to go:

> Up to the mountain's top,
> And mark the musical confusion
> Of hounds and echo in conjunction

> (Act IV, Sc. 1, 110)

and he has chosen a wife who shares his own tastes. His pride is in his 'flew'd and sanded' hounds, 'bred out of the Spartan kind'. And when he cannot be hunting he requires some other 'sport' (Act V, Sc. 1, 42, 90) with which 'to ease the anguish of a torturing hour'.

Hippolyta

She is for the most part a silent actor in the play. She takes her place with dignity as a soldier queen by the side of her soldier husband that is to be. She betrays no youthful longing for the rapid flight of time (Act I, Sc. 1, 7-11), nor does she often address her future lord in endearing terms. We can hardly imagine her ever to have had a very close connection with the fairy world, although Titania speaks of her to Oberon as 'your buskin'd mistress, and your warrior love'. The remarks she makes during the performance of the Interlude – 'This is the silliest stuff that ever I heard', 'I am aweary of this moon; would he would change', 'such a Pyramus', and 'I hope she will be brief' – are hardly such as might tend to the encouragement of the actors – supposing them to be so commonplace as to require encouragement; but this we may perhaps excuse in her, remembering that she has been until now a stranger to the civilization of Athens.

Hermia

At first Hermia is the typical young girl in love against her father's wishes. Perhaps we have a slight clue that a real person lies behind this stock exterior when she promises to meet Lysander ''By all the vows that ever men have broke/(In number more than ever women spoke).'' This remark has life and reality, especially in the light of what follows. In itself, too, it has a spark of originality – she could have just sworn on her life the way Lysander is always doing. When the play has progressed to the height of love's confusion,

Hermia emerges as very distinct indeed. She is dark and small, but quick-tempered even to fierceness. Though she and Helena may once have been almost two persons in one body as they sat in girlish companionship, under the pressure of being a woman bereft of her man this twinship is sundered and each girl emerges as a separate personality. Driven almost to madness by Lysander's unaccountable rejection of her, Hermia asks exactly the right question, "Am not I Hermia? are not you Lysander?"

The men, who are not in control at all, keep avowing their new-found sanity and sobriety. But Hermia, who remains constant throughout, sees her very identity at stake. Her awareness of this question is itself an assertion of her identity so that when she gets her Lysander back she gets more than just that. She gets herself back too in an increased way by having felt the basis of her identity threatened. Hermia does not say anything during the performance of the play. In fact, her last words are in Act IV, Scene 1, when she says she feels as if she were seeing double. One cannot say for sure, but perhaps Hermia's silence in the rest of the play indicates that the experience she had in the wood did have a permanent, beneficial effect. Perhaps Shakespeare is telling us by this that she knows better now than to do as Lysander and Demetrius do. But this must remain a conjecture, for the fabric of the play will not support weighty contentions. Puck makes certain that the gossamer veil remains between us and all that has passed before us on the stage – he says to consider it all a dream. And behind the sheer gossamer, everything shimmers brightly, but it perforce remains tantalizingly indistinct.

Helena

Helena is the love-sick, love-lorn maiden. She is tall and fair, and until events conspire against her, she droops and pines beautifully all over her cruel beloved. She does show some measure of initiative when she betrays her best friend so that she can gain her own ends with her boy friend. And her persistent, abject humility is certainly remarkable. When she suddenly finds herself beloved of two instead of by none, she is forced out of her accustomed role. She is full of self-pity at this discomfort – she's much more adept at being love-lorn through long habit. Perhaps she sees herself as quite pretty at pining and pleading, pale and slender as she is. Anyway, her immediate reaction is to suspect a plot, and she pities herself all the more. Her chief defense is that her plight deserves pity, not scorn. This attitude remains intact for a time. She deploys it artfully to upbraid Hermia, saying that the latter shamefully betrays their long and fast friendship. How can Hermia be so cruel to such a sweet, dear, faithful, trusting friend, and one who has had such a hard time of it already? But when Hermia's temper flares, things look a little different. Now Helena remembers an action a little at variance with the earlier idyllic portrayal of her relationship with Hermia. In fact, she confesses that she betrayed her friend's confidence and told the person who would most like to spoil the elopement all about it. A little later it is revealed by the frightened Helena that things weren't so rosy back in the good old days either. In fact, Helena's opinion is that Hermia was a fierce vixten at school.

So, under pressure Helena ventures out a little more on her own too. She actually gathers her drooping, love-sick self together enough to run away from Hermia. Fear of bodily harm from her little friend replaces the piteous sorow with which she withstood all manner of threats from Demetrius. This abandonment of her initial role is a step forward toward an individual personality. Running from Hermia interests us much more than her running after Demetrius. Helena, too, says no more after Act IV, Scene 1, and her comment there is quite perceptive. She says she can't feel secure about Demetrius – it's like finding a jewel by lucky accident. We who know Demetrius's true state couldn't have said it any better. And so, though we must leave this as mere conjecture for the same reason as we did for Hermia, we can't deny that somehow Helena knows what she's getting when she gets Demetrius.

Lysander

The lover of Hermia, is spoken of as 'a worthy gentleman', of high rank and good fortune. Before the play opens he has impressed his image firmly upon Hermia's fancy and being secure in the possession of her love, he treats his future father-in-law with some scorn (Act I, Sc. 1, 93-5).

He must not be thought faithless because, owing to Puck's blunder he came under the influence of 'Cupid's flower' and suddenly transferred his affections to Helena.

Demetrius

Demetrius differs from Lysander in character only in one important respect. He was inconstant and sinned through faithlessness to his betrothed Helena. The supernatural power of the fairies was needed in order to restore him to his 'natural taste', and then, having returned to his first love he remembers his breach of faith only as youthful playfulness (Act IV, Sc. 1, 165-77).

Demetrius has the dubious distinction of being the one character in the play who remains enchanted. Thus when he is so loud-mouthed in his superior scorn of the "Pyramus and Thisbe" play, we do notice him especially. We think, who is he to mock this earnest endeavor as foolish, and this questioning of his identity is our primary reaction to him as a character.

Egeus

The father of Hermia, Egeus is the typical disgruntled father whose daughter is silly enough to love whom she wants, not whom he wants. The first words we hear him speak establish him as this kind of character. He says he's "full of vexation" at Hermia, and the reasons he gives are the typical response of the older, stolid generation to young and wayward love. Egeus is a man to whom the accouterments of love are just stuff and nonsense. Balconies by moonlight, love poetry, souvenirs, gifts of jewelry, dowers, and candy are all a silly nuisance in his opinion. All they do is interfere with the orderly, business-like fulfillment by a dutiful daughter of a marriage contract made by a responsible father. Egeus is the embodiment of this classic attitude toward love and marriage. He would rather see his daughter dead or shut up in a nunnery than married to someone he hasn't chosen for her.

Bottom

Nick Bottom the weaver is one of Shakespeare's most memorable creations. When we first meet him, the play of "Pyramus and Thisbe" is being cast. Bottom is ready to take on anything. He has complete confidence in his ability to sweep from one end of the emotional scale to the other. The energy and enthusiasm with which he participates in life are immediately evident. Some critics have objected to what they consider his domineering, brash, self-centered personality, but this is a gross misunderstanding. When he shares Titania's bower, his easy graciousness with his extraordinary new companions is a mark of his marvelous ability to adapt immediately to whatever life offers him. His energetic love of life, his naïveté and eager innocence obtain his entrance into this other-world so different from his own. And he enjoys it to the fullest. When Bottom awakens from his "dream," his own manner of reacting to it is the best approach to the experience. Wonder, awe, and a strong sense of the power beyond man's apprehension are communicated by his words there. He rightly declares the unfathomability of his "dream" and feels most profoundly its power. He knows that it should be called "Bottom's Dream" for these correct reasons. Starting from his position as a rock-bottom realist, Bottom can, with the same vigor and joy he brings to whatever he does, respond to this power and believe.

The fantastically transformed Bottom, seemingly the least likely candidate in all the world before his transformation, becomes a participator in the fairy world in the incredible role of Titania's beloved. But we see thus that it was possible after all; indeed it seems an absolutely necessary liaison once we see how naturally Bottom takes it. He conducts himself with such sobriety and yet such grace, with his own good sense and yet with such enjoyment that we see he is a weaver in this deeper sense too – Bottom the weaver is supremely capable of uniting these disparate worlds. His very person embodies the union of reality and illusion, carrying as he does Puck's trick on his real, sturdy shoulders. His love of life enables him to engage in it to the fullest. The fullness of his engagement unites experience. In this play where love and art and dreams assert their power over life, Bottom embodies the union of reality and illusion wherein lie the secret springs and mysterious force of life itself.

Peter Quince, Francis Flute, Tom Snout, Snug, Robin Starveling

These worthy, simple men pursue various trades in Athens. Quince is a carpenter, Snout is a tinker, Flute is a bellows-mender, Snug is a joiner, Starveling is a tailor. They are Bottom's companions and together with him they prepare and present the play of "Pyramus and Thisbe" as a wedding entertainment at Theseus' and the lovers' marriages. We laugh at these "hempen homespuns" (as Puck calls them), at their blunders with language, and at their inept theatrical venture. But we are shown that they love Bottom and he loves them. We feel the warmth and reality of these characters and admire their simple earnestness. They are far less foolish than those who mock them as fools. And they perform the valuable service in this play of highlighting this last fact.

Oberon

The King of the Fairies has the majesty and power in his world that Theseus has in his. The difference between the two worlds bespeaks the difference between the two characters, for Oberon is triumphant in poetry and illusion – "King of Shadows" Puck calls him, while as mere shadows Theseus disparages even the most expert purveyors of illusion (Act V, Sc. 1, 212-213). The marriage of Theseus is the framing event in the daylight world of the play. It is the first thing we hear of and the last thing that happens, but the cloth that is woven within this frame is of Oberon's design. He and his assistant Puck move the shuttle of this loom madly between the straight uprights of Theseus' frame. The lovers are matched as warp and woof, and Bottom's experience runs as a strong diagonal thread knitting all sturdily.

All this comes about because Oberon can't have something that he wants. Titania has a changeling whom she has excellent reasons for wishing to keep. The little boy's mother was a special friend who died giving birth to this child. But Oberon must have this boy. He obtains the love juice to divert Titania's interest from the child and he'll only disenchant her once the changeling is securely in his own train. When we remember that this is the motive behind all that happens in the woods, Oberon comes off little better than the two male lovers. For magnanimity of spirit and depth of emotion he's about on a par with them. However, as soon as Oberon speaks the poetry Shakespeare has given him, we too are completely in his power. His magnificent description of the occasion when he first saw "the little western flower" obliterates any lingering doubts about the petty purpose he intends it for. His poetry evokes a music that made "the rude sea" grow civil and caused the stars to shoot "madly from their spheres." This is the Oberon we remember, the King of Shadows to whom such things happen and who can thus recreate his experiences.

Titania

The Queen of Fairies carries herself with the nobility and dignity befitting her station. When Oberon tries to bully her into giving up her changeling, she stands up to him with admirable spirit and we feel she has the right on her side. But the action which does most to create her as a character in our eyes is of a very different nature. Charmed by the love juice, Titania coddles and caresses Bottom. This appears highly ridiculous to Oberon and Puck, but somehow it increases her stature in our eyes. We can't help but like her better for it. First, we have affection for Bottom and he reacts beautifully to his new and completely foreign situation. In addition, Titania does not lower herself – she treats him well and wants to make him a pure spirit like herself. The effect of all this is that though she is the female counterpart of Oberon in many ways, the woman in her also plays a part in our conception of her character.

Puck

This mischievous elf is unique unto himself. There is no way to describe him, except in his own words. He tells us he loves preposterous things best and he delights no end in the pranks he executes in this play. He is a homey, rustic spirit. His language and the kind of mischief he specializes in demonstrate this. Though Oberon is his master, Puck is immediately responsible for the confusions. It is he who mistakes Lysander for Demetrius and puts the ass's head on Bottom. And it is also he who suggests to us that perhaps the whole play is nothing but a dream.

Peaseblossom, Cobweb, Moth, Mustardseed

The fairies in *A Midsummer Night's Dream* are Shakespeare's invention. There had, of course, been fairies in English folklore, but Shakespeare's differ in several important respects from these. It is Shakespeare's fairies as depicted in this play which have held sway over the public imagination ever since their creation, replacing those of folk tradition. Shakespeare's differ from the latter in three outstanding ways: their diminutive size, their association with flowers, and their benevolent natures. The fairy of folklore had none of these characteristics. The popular conception that has prevailed has them because it is derived from Shakespeare's creation in this play. The names of the above fairies in particular are in keeping with the tiny, airy, delicate creatures Shakespeare has created. The activities that Titania assigns to them paint an extraordinary scene of the whimsical, delightful, non-mortal world that is brought into being in this play.

Philostrate

This minor character is in charge of providing entertainment at Duke Theseus' court. All we know about him is that he thinks the workmen's play is unworthy to be seen, and says it is "nothing, nothing in the world." Theseus sent Philostrate out to prepare entertainment at the very beginning, just as Oberon sent Puck to fetch the love juice. The different between the two lieutenants is in keeping with the different between the two masters. Philostrate is not characterized at all fully, but he does serve to complete a certain pleasing symmetry.

Theme

The theme of *A Midsummer Night's Dream* is that "love hath no law but his own," is blind, unreasonable, unpredictable, inconstant; that "all's fair in love and war." But since it is an entertaining fantasy, neither realistic nor truly tragic even for a moment, we must not take its romantic moments too seriously; in fact, we shall find that they are themselves made fun of, reflected in the distorting mirror of farce.

Practically everything that is said and done in the play, whether by the dignified Theseus and Hippolyta, the mixed-up young lovers, the exquisite, delicate, not-quite-human fairies (Robin Goodfellow excepted), or the low comedians (Bottom excepted) is related to this theme, so that the whole is a network of parallel, circling, or crisscrossing threads which somehow form a satisfying pattern. Or, if we think of the parts separately, it is like a piece of music in which a single motif is repeated in different keys and tempos.

Theseus, though he loves Hippolyta and will wed her in another key, has won her love doing her injuries. Hermia for love of Lysander defies her father and Athenian law. Demetrius makes vows of love to Helena and then to Hermia. Hermia, wooed by two young men who in the eyes of the world are indistinguishably handsome, rich, and well-born, dotes upon one and hardly knows that the other exists. Demetrius, who has courted Helena and eventually marries her, hates her for a time, is sick when he does look on her, and spurns her with his foot. She, for a few hours of his disdainful company, betrays the secret of her dearest friend.

We are not told whether or not the artisans have wives or sweethearts. They *are* obsessed by the dream of moving an audience with a tragedy on the theme of obsessive love.

Oberon and Titania, though they are lord and lady and eventually rejoin in amity, are jealous of one another over Oberon's straying after nymphs and admiring Hippolyta, and Titania's doting on Theseus to the point of helping him in his earlier love affairs with mortal women. Their quarrel is reflected in the unseasonable weather on earth and in the young lovers' quarrel which follows the transfer of Lysander's affection, and Titania's melting fondness for Bottom mirrors in ridiculous fashion the doting of Hermia and Helena and of all mortals who lavish affection on unworthy objects. Only the stability of the mature and noble Duke, who does not believe in fairies and distrusts the excesses of lovers almost as much as those of lunatics and poets, introduces order into the pattern and brings all right in the end. The interlude, possibly a burlesque of love tragedies like *Romeo and Juliet*, is ridiculed for inept performance but tacitly approved in principle.

Of love itself, we may distinguish three kinds: the passionate, headstrong love of youth, the mature love of older people with responsibilities, in whom passion is subordinated to duty, and the ephemeral love of the fairies with their petty quarrels and reconciliations. Tying these kinds of love together is the theme of change and transformation. Shakespeare repeatedly reminds us that love has not to do with constancy, but rather with change.

Points of Interest
Lawlessness and Laughableness Of Love

All the love stories present extravagant types of love. Theseus, in putting the lunatic, the lover, and the poet into one class "of imagination all compact," is satirizing love as a type of lunacy in those afflicted with it. Since the play was written for laughable entertainment at a happy occasion, this characteristic of love is stressed over and over in references and examples.

Humor

Bottom is the nearest approach to the stage clown, who in most plays is the source of humor. He supplies it in his bumptious character, his misuse of words, his acting, and his sense of equality with Titania and the Duke and the Duchess. The five other tradesmen contribute to it to a lesser extent. The difficulties that arise from Puck's charms and mistakes supply humorous situations rather than humor itself, and are more entertaining than laughable in their seriousness.

Spectacular

This element of interest is presented chiefly in the attributes and nonsense of a masque. The most striking situation is the unexpected appearance of Bottom with an ass's head on his shoulders. The fairies demand attention in their swift movements, gay costumes, and unusual doings. The tradesmen's play, actions, and incongruity probably leave a more lasting impression on the mind of the spectator than any other portion of the play. Nearly all the scenes occur in a wood on a moonlit night, adding weirdness and a sense of romance.

Song and Dance

Song is indicated in the stage directions only three times. The first, when the fairies sing Titania to sleep before Oberon anoints her eyes; the second when Bottom awakens her; and the third as they all bless the newly married couples. But many of the frequent tetrameters may easily be included with the others. Special music is called for several times. The movements of the attendant fairies and Puck are always in dancing. Oberon and Titania dance together after their reconciliation, and again in their closing performance in the palace. The boisterous and clumsy dance or bergomask of the two clowns after the play is a parody on that of the fairies and may be made very amusing in its contrast.

Contrast

This device figures largely: maturity and self-control in the royal couple and youth and passion in the young lovers; daintiness and immateriality in the fairies and crudeness and materialism in the tradesmen; the comedy and dignity in the main story and tragedy and the ridiculous in the interlude. Contrast reaches its height in the bringing together of Titania and Bottom. Throughout the play we note the constant contrast between reality and illusion.

Supernatural

The introduction of fairies accords with what was then a common belief in their existence and in their powers concerning the directing of human affairs. They add an atmosphere of comedy, charm, lightness and relief. Oberon is careful to draw a distinction between fairies and ghosts, to ensure that his natural kindliness will not be confused with the malignancy of other spirits.

Dramatic Irony

When a speaker's words convey to his listeners a meaning that he does not comprehend, since they are aware of facts of which he is ignorant, the double meaning is called dramatic irony. We find this situation all through the misunderstandings of the lovers, since only the audience knows the effect of the charms underlying them. The same occurs in Titania's deception in Bottom, and still further in Bottom's ignorance of his ass's head. To a lesser extent we find it in the interlude, in which the clowns believe in their excellence and fail to understand their critical audience.

Anachronisms

An anachronism is a false relation of an event, a person, a scene, language – in fact anything – to a time when that event or thing or person was either not in existence, or could not possibly have happened. Shakespeare was never particularly concerned with insignificant details, and this is especially evident in *A Midsummer Night's Dream*. For in dreams, "bright visitants wander through gardens of unearthly flowers, and a primitive creature re-arises in bloody gambol there, on whom time has shed its centuries in vain." Therefore, we should not be surprised to find that in this play whole scenes are anachronistic, as well as innumerable allusions.

The Interlude

Besides the unsuitability of the actors to their parts, the ridiculous antics during its performance, the bad rendition of Prologue, the breaking down of Moonshine, and the exchange of remarks between the players and the audience (which in those days was a common occurrence when the important spectators sat on the sides of the stage), the following faults contribute to humor:

1. Defective rhymes: plain and certain; sinister and whisper.

2. Incorrect classical allusions: Shefalus and Procrus for Cephalus and Procris; Lemander and Helen for Leander and Hero; Thisby for Thisbe.

3. Excess of exclamations: "O night; O wall; O sweet; O lovely wall!"

4. Padding to fill out the meter: "did scare away, or rather did affright; O night! alack, alack, alack!"

5. Abuse of alliterations: "bravely broach'd his boiling bloody breast."

6. Pathos: the ludicrous treatment of a serious theme throughout.

The Fairy Court

PURPOSES   (1) The fairies put in concrete form the poetic, romantic, irresponsible, and delusive world in which human beings in love exist. (2)

They interest the audience in illustrating graphically a theory in the nature of their beings, their interests, and their relation to mankind. (3) They add variety in their music, song, and dance, the spectacular in costume and scenic effects, and charm in daintiness and diminutiveness.

ORGANIZATION   They form an organized court with a king and his jester, a queen and attendants, and subjects, referred to as elves. Their home is in the farthest steppes of India, to which they return shortly after dawn from other parts of the world. The king and his page concern themselves chiefly with adventures with mortals and the coarser four-footed animals, while the queen and her court are more interested in feminine accomplishments with flowers, harmless animals and dancing.

DESCRIPTION   They are exceedingly small, Titania dressing in the cast slough of a snake, and the elves hide in acorns and use butterfly wings for fans. They move with exceeding swiftness, disappearing for ''the third part of a minute'' or girdling the earth in forty minutes. They form one of the elements of nature, becoming invisible when necessary, holding the seasons in subjection, adorning flowers, silencing mice and snakes, and controlling disturbing or dangerous animals.

WORK   Titania's attendants prepare her bower and provide food, clothing, and entertainment. Oberon watches over mortals from Queen Elizabeth to the four Athenians. Puck carries out his master's commands, but more frequently delights in playing pranks on people who do not meet with his approval.

Time Sequence

The first printed edition (1600) had neither scene nor act divisions. The First Folio text (1623) had acts but no scenes. Modern editors have divided the action into nine scenes and assigned their locations, easily deducible from the dialogue, as follows: *Athens. The Palace of Theseus,* Act I, Scene 1 and Act V, Scene 1; *Athens. Quince's house,* Act I, Scene 2 and Act IV, Scene 2; *A wood near Athens,* Act II, Scene 1; *Another part of the wood,* Act II, Scene 2 and Act III, Scene 1; *Another part of the wood,* namely a ''haunted grove'', Act III, Scene 2 and Act IV, Scene 1. The movements of the characters from place to place were presumably suggested on stage by rapid exits and re-entrances.

The allusions to night, day, and time in general in the course of the action are frequently found to be inconsistent when scrutinized with the aid of a calendar, though the impressions of elapsed time and of continuity are rarely if ever lacking for the audience during a performance. Theseus says (Act I, Sc. 1, 2) that four days and four nights will precede the wedding, which should therefore occur on the fifth day. But Hermia and Lysander (Act I, Sc. 1, 164) and the actors (Act I, Sc. 2, 105-106) agree to meet *to-morrow night,* so that Act II, Act III, and part of Act IV occupy the second day and night. At Act IV, Scene 1, 97 Robin hears the morning lark, and at Act IV, Scene 1, 138 we learn that this, the third day, is the wedding day. In the afternoon Bottom rejoins his fellows and Act V takes place that evening. The moon is a stage moon and despite Bottom's insistence that they consult the almanac to "find out moonshine" (Act III, Sc. 1, 53-55), no correspondence to the processes of the earth satellite is to be expected.

A Contrast Between *A Midsummer Night's Dream* and *The Tempest*

The contrast between *A Midsummer Night's Dream* and *The Tempest* is of particular interest to the student of Shakespeare, because it enables him to perceive some of the striking differences between the poet's earlier and later methods. Both plays are irregular in form, and have in them something of the nature of a masque. In both the influence of Ovid is seen, and in both fairies play a very prominent part. But here the resemblance ends.

The Tempest displays quite a different mood in the poet. In *A Midsummer Night's Dream* all is bright and fresh, full of fascinating poetry without any very deep thought running through it. In the later play (*The Tempest*) we can see Shakespeare, as Dr. Dowden expresses it, 'tenderly bending over the joys and sorrows of youth'. In the earlier play the poet writes from the point of view of one who enters zealously into the feelings of youth, taking life not too seriously, smiling at the perplexities and entanglements caused by the mischievous sprite Puck, and enjoying the absurdities of the unimaginative Athenian swains; but in *The Tempest* he has a more serious purpose in view than merely to amuse or delight. He has a lesson to enforce. He teaches mankind the lesson of duty. In *A Midsummer Night's Dream* Oberon's attendant Puck plays his pranks simply for the fun of the thing, and laughs at the pain or embarrassment he causes. Ariel, on the other hand, in *The Tempest* is well-mannered and sensitive, 'a minister of retribution, who is touched with the sense of pity at the woes he inflicts'. Puck is the familiar Robin Goodfellow with an extra strain of poetry infused into his composition; Ariel is the pure creation of the poet. In *A Midsummer Night's Dream* the fairies are half irresponsible actors in whose hands 'human mortals' are mere puppets, but in *The Tempest* the fairies themselves are ministers of the powerful human will of their superior, Prospero.

A Midsummer Night's Dream: Critical Appraisal

"I know not why Shakespeare calls this play a Midsummer-Night's Dream, when he so carefully informs us that it happened on the night preceding *May* day," wrote Dr. Johnson almost two hundred years ago.[1] There have been surprisingly few attempts in the interval to supply an answer. Most of them came from Johnson's contemporaries. "I imagine that the title of this play was suggested by the time it was first introduced on the stage, which was probably at *Midsummer*. 'A Dream for the entertainment of a Midsummernight.' *Twelfth Night* and *The Winter's Tale* had probably their title from a similar circumstance,'' wrote Malone.[2] And Steevens: ''In *Twelfth Night*, Act III, Scene 4, Olivia observes of Malvolio's seeming frenzy, that 'it is a very *Midsummer* madness.' That time of the year we may therefore suppose was anciently thought productive of mental vagaries resembling the scheme of Shakespeare's play. To this circumstance it might have owed its title.''[3] In the nineteenth century we have to look to Germany for a discussion of the problem. Tieck, after giving Malone's explanation, adds that . . . [it is only during this night that many plants and flowers attain their full strength and any magical powers – ED.'s TRANS.].[4] Simrock declared that *A Midsummer Night's Dream* was a title which cannot have come from Shakespeare, and defiantly entitled his translation of the play *Walpurgisnachtstraum*. In our own century several more explanations have been offered. Sir Edmund Chambers finds the significance of the title in Puck's invitation to the audience to regard the whole play as a dream. ''It is life seen through a glass darkly; such a vision of life as a man might have on the Midsummer Night, the one season of the year around which Elizabethan superstition gathered most closely, when herbs were believed to have their especial virtues, and strange beings to be abroad.''[5] Walter De la Mare completes the range of conjectures by surmising that the title may be due to the fact ''that 'on such a night' the happy notion of it stole into Shakespeare's mind,'' [6] thus making the dreamer the poet himself.

None of these explanations are mutually exclusive. But most of them merely shift the problem. For we are now left to explain why Shakespeare should have chosen the eve of Mayday for the action of most of his play, rather than Midsummer Night. Both nights are well fitted to provide the time-setting for the supernatural events in the wood, for they are the two nights of the year when fairies were thought to be particularly powerful and when magic and every form of witchcraft was believed to be practised. But there are three associations which the eve of Mayday did not share with Midsummer Night: that of flower magic, the notion being that certain herbs and flowers gathered on that night possessed various wonder-working powers; that of lovers' dreams; and that of madness. The explanations, therefore, which seem to me most plausible are those of Steevens, Tieck, and Chambers. Of these Steevens's seems the most important. For love-madness is the central theme of *A Midsummer Night's Dream*. It is this which ties together various sections of the play, from Demetrius's transfer of affection from Helena to Hermia and then back to Helena, to Titania's temporary love for Bottom. The theme has both a prologue and an epilogue, in each of which it receives a generalized formulation. The prologue is found in Helena's soliloquy in Act I, the epilogue in Theseus's speech on the lunatic, the lover, and the poet in Act V.

Now happy some o'er other some can be!
Through Athens I am thought as fair as she,

But what of that? Demetrius thinks not so:
He will not know what all but he do know.
And as he errs, doting on Hermia's eyes,
So I, admiring of his qualities . . .
Things base and vile, holding no quantity,
Love can transpose to form and dignity.
Love looks not with the eyes, but with the mind:
And therefore is winged Cupid painted blind.
Nor hath Love's mind of any judgement taste:
Wings and no eyes figure unheedy haste.
And therefore is Love said to be a child:
Because in choice he is so oft beguiled.

(Act I, Sc. 1, 226 ff.)

The love described here is cut off both from the evidence of the senses, which it belies, and from the corrective power of judgment. It is purely a creature of the imagination, of "seething brains," a kind of madness, in which the victim may be intellectually aware of his illusion but unable to resist it:

And as he errs, doing on Hermia's eyes,
So I, admiring of his qualities.

It is a love which has no basis in reality, which creates a phantom, a mere shadow of the beloved person; it is a dream. Though it is entirely devoid of judgment the victim is, ironically, under the delusion that he is following reason in his choice. When Lysander, under the power of the love-philter, has been made to transfer his love from Hermia to Helena, he exclaims:

The will of man is by his reason swayed;
And reason says you are the worthier maid.
Things growing are not ripe until their season:
So I, being young, till now ripe not to reason –
And touching now the point of human skill,
Reason becomes the marshal to my will,
And leads me to your eyes; where I o'erlook
Love's stories, written in love's richest book.

(Act II, Sc. 2, 123 ff.)

This love is wholly due to the whims of Cupid.

Cupid is a knavish lad,
Thus to make poor females mad,

exclaims Puck when moved to pity by the sufferings of the two maidens (Act III, Sc. 2, 440-1). Oberon, in his use of the love-philter, merely usurps the function of Cupid, but instead of the love-god's aimless and wilful exercise of his power turns them towards beneficent as well as selfish ends. It is a controlled exercise of Cupid's power but its effects are exactly the same, whether produced by love-juice or golden arrow: the eyes are blinded, the judgment is disabled, and reason is put to flight. Former love is turned to loathing, former loathing to love.

Shakespeare next shows us the *reductio ad absurdum* of this love-madness in the Bottom-Titania love scenes. Here, in the infatuation of the Queen of fairies for a weaver metamorphosed into an ass, we have displayed the full absurdity of the kind of love which is engendered in the imagination only, uncorrected by judgment and the senses. Bottom himself points the moral of the situation. To Titania's impassioned declaration of love,

> I pray thee, gentle mortal, sing again!
> Mine ear is much enamoured of thy note . . .
> So is mine eye enthralled to thy shape,
> And thy fair virtue's force – perforce – doth move me,
> On the first view, to say, to swear, I love thee,
> (Act III, Sc. 1, 130 ff.)

he replies:

> Methinks, mistress, you should have little reason for that.
> And yet, to say the truth, reason and love keep little
> company together now-a-days. The more the pity, that some
> honest neighbors will not make them friends. Nay, I can
> gleek upon occasion.

In the relationship of Theseus and Hippolyta reason and love have been made friends and keep company together. Hence it is fitting that the final summing up of the theme of love-madness should be entrusted to Theseus in his famous speech about the lunatic, the lover, and the poet. The lines on the poet, as Professor Dover Wilson was the first to point out,[7] appear to have been added by Shakespeare as an afterthought. But while they are for us the most interesting part of the speech and also contain the best verse, they do obscure its original purpose. For we are left chiefly with the impression of the poet as a madman, while Shakespeare's earlier intention was to make us see the lover in this role, clinching the identification of love and madness which has been suggested throughout the play.

While the theme of love-madness weaves together various apparently unrelated portions of *A Midsummer Night's Dream*, Shakespeare creates unity of atmosphere chiefly by flooding the play with moonlight. There is only one daylight scene in the entire play, part of the first scene of Act IV, where we watch the coming of dawn and with it the arrival of Theseus's hunting party. And here the coming of daylight and the sounding of the hunting horns announce the return of sanity, the dispersal of magic and illusion, the end of the dream. Theseus and Hippolyta are both daylight characters. Neither of them is unimaginative, and Theseus, at least, is depicted as an ardent lover. But he has wooed Hippolyta with his sword, in a fashion very different from Lysander's wooing of Hermia, of which Egeus tells him:

Thou hast by moonlight at her window sung,
With feigning voice, verses of feigning love.

(Act I, Sc. 1, 30)

And the Duke's cool reason and good sense throw into relief the lovers' absurdities. They have their natural existence by moonlight, which propagates phantoms and illusions, the world of dreams.

In this play we are given three wholly distinct kinds of fairies, provided we can speak of Puck as a fairy at all. He was not considered so in popular superstitition, but was thought of as a spirit of another sort, whose merry pranks made him the favorite among all the sprites that haunted the English countryside. In our play he considers himself to be a fairy, as his "And we fairies, that do run by the triple Hecate's team" (Act V, Sc. 1, 381) shows. He is the complete opposite of the tiny fairies with whom Shakespeare fills Titania's train, being gross and earthy, boisterous, rough, and boyish, where the tiny fairies are aerial, timid, and courteous. Nothing could be more misleading than to speak of them as irresponsible children, as some critics do. They are conscientious and very much overworked servants of the queen, with little time for idle gossiping. In their encounters with Bottom the tiny fairies, so far from being like children, show themselves accomplished and ceremonious courtiers. To see them otherwise robs the scene of much of its humor. For Bottom, with his customary adaptability to any part he is called upon to play, at once fits himself to his new role of Prince Consort, and proceeds to hold a levee. As we would expect, he plays the part to perfection. He is courteous without condescension, well informed about each fairy's family, genuinely interested in their affairs. In his second encounter with them we find the same qualities, mingled with greater familiarity. Now we have, "Scratch my head, Peaseblossom," but also, "Give me your neaf, Monsieur Mustardseed. Pray you, leave your curtsy, good monsieur"

(Act IV, Sc. 1, 6 ff.).

Oberon and Titania, though very different from the attendant fairies, are no more childlike or irresponsible than they. When commentators speak of "little Titania," or when one critic, lamenting the undomesticated life led by Oberon and Titania, tells us that "acorn-cups impose no fellowship,"[8] it is evident that they take the King and Queen of fairyland to be of the same miniature brand as their attendant spirits. That Shakespeare did not think of them in that way is plain enough. Not only would it be unactable to have a tiny Titania make love to Bottom, but it would also be unthinkable. For much of the humor of their love scenes depends on our realization that it is a supremely beautiful woman who is enamored of this weaver turned ass. (Had Shakespeare thought of the fairy queen as diminutive, "Titania" would have been a most unhappy choice of name for her.) Shakespeare clearly thinks of Titania and Oberon as of the same stature as the traditional English fairies, who were believed to be of normal human height or slightly below it. Nor are they depicted as ethereal, mere gossamer and moonlight. Not only Titania's

"Sleep thou, and I will wind thee in my arms" (Act IV, Sc. 1, 39), but also Oberon's

> Come, my queen, take hands with me,
> And rock the ground whereon these sleepers be
> (Act IV, Sc. 1, 84)

make against this impression.

But more harmful than the notion of Oberon's and Titania's diminutive size is the notion of their childlikeness and irresponsibility. Of this I can find no trace in the play. They are the counterpart in the spirit-world of Theseus and Hippolyta, like them full of stateliness, but more ceremonious and distant. Their quarrel is not a children's squabble, no sooner engaged in than forgotten, as Sir Edmund Chambers would have us believe, [9] but a quarrel which has been in progress for many months, disrupting the whole body politic of fairyland. Only thus can we understand Titania's speech about the chaos in nature, which has arisen out of their quarrel (Act II, Sc. 1, 82 ff.). It is more than merely a topical allusion to an unusually bad English summer. It rather portrays the disorder in the macrocosm which, in so many of Shakespeare's plays, accompanies disorder in the body politic, here the state of fairydom.

Shakespeare has sometimes been reproached with having gelded the English fairy, with having robbed it of its fearfulness and hence its reality, and turned it into a trifle light as air, the mere plaything of the imagination. We can see why he should have done so for the purposes of this play. He probably felt that the traditional English fairy was too uncanny and fearful a creature to be accommodated in this scene of tragical mirth. And so, in creating the attendant fairies in this play, he drew on a *jeu d'esprit* written probably a few months earlier, Mercutio's Queen Mab speech in *Romeo and Juliet*. But the miniature and flower-like fairies had been created for a special purpose in a particular play and in no way ousted the traditional English fairy from the poet's imagination. Not until *The Tempest* does he return to the "Shakespearian" fairy; all the references in the intervening plays are to the conventional fairies of English folklore.

By Ernest Schanzer

Notes

1. Boswell's Variorum edition (1821), vol. 5, p. 296, n. 3.
2. *Ibid*.
3. *Ibid*.
4. Notes to Schlegel's Translation, vol. 3, p. 352.
5. *Shakespeare: A Survey* (1935), p. 83.
6. *Pleasures and Speculations* (1940), p. 275.
7. New Shakespeare ed. *A Midsummer-Night's Dream*, pp. 80 ff.
8. H. B. Charlton, *Shakespearean Comedy* (1938), p. 117.
9. *op. cit.*, p. 85.

Shadow and Substance in
A Midsummer Night's Dream

A Midsummer Night's Dream is another of Shakespeare's early comedies. The frequently artificial verse and the shallow characterization of some of the major protagonists are signs of immaturity in the dramatist. But in stage technique the play is a masterpiece. Both implicitly, through the way in which Shakespeare skilfully intertwines his plots, and explicitly, in the comments which are made in the play on the relationship between art and reality, *A Midsummer Night's Dream* reveals its author's concern with the function and purpose of drama and the interaction of the playwright and his public.

Most remarkable about the play is the way in which it presents several planes of reality and we may well begin by considering what these various planes are and how and by which characters they are represented.

A Midsummer Night's Dream was probably written to be performed at an Elizabethan wedding. Though we have no external documentary proof of this, the subject matter and the manner of the play are themselves sufficient evidence to support the theory. In this respect, *A Midsummer Night's Dream* may be compared with *Love's Labour Lost* and *The Tempest,* which also contain a kind of built-in tribute to the original spectators and reference to the hymeneal nature of the original occasion for which they were first written or soon after adapted. So we may begin by envisaging a play by the successful, up-and-coming William Shakespeare being performed by the Lord Chamberlain's Men before an audience of guests gathered together in the great hall of an Elizabethan mansion to celebrate the wedding of an Elizabethan nobleman, the master of the house.

The play which the company presented on that summer evening at the end of the sixteenth-century is composed of several strands, all woven together within one frame-work. The framework is that of a royal wedding, between Duke Theseus of Athens and Hippolyta, Queen of the Amazons. When the play opens four days remain before the wedding celebrations. In the two-hour interim we (like Shakespeare's original audience) have watched the working out of the several themes which together constitute the major action of Shakespeare's play.

The first theme is that of four lovers, Lysander and Hermia, Helena and Demetrius. Hermia, sought in marriage by Demetrius, the beloved of Helena, prefers Lysander, who returns her love. But her father insists that she marry Demetrius and she is granted four days in which to decide whether she will bow to her father's will or suffer the bitter alternative laid down by Athenian law – death or retirement to a nunnery. The day of the royal wedding is the day on which Hermia must give her answer and so the story of the lovers is at once bound to the framework by the dramatic unity of time.

The second theme is that of the quarrel between Oberon, King of the

Fairies, and his queen Titania. She has in her possession an Indian changeling whom Oberon longs to have among his train of followers but whom Titania refuses to relinquish. The fairy monarchs meet in the woods outside Athens because each has come to bestow a blessing on the royal couple and it further appears, from their mutual accusations, that there had formerly been amorous ties between Theseus and Titania, Oberon and Hippolyta. Oberon, intent on punishing Titania by tricking her into falling in love with some beast that she may encounter in the night, is fortuitously able also to assist the four lovers who are wandering in the wood by putting the love-in-idleness lotion to good use in straightening out their tangled affections. In this way, the fairy-theme, already linked with the royal wedding by the unity of place, is also linked with the theme of the four human lovers.

It is also, however, linked with the third theme, that of the Athenian artisans, who, preparing an entertainment to be performed before the royal couple at their wedding, choose the woods outside Athens as a suitable place for an uninterrupted rehearsal. For it is one of these artisans, transformed by Puck into a monstrous apparition of a human body crowned with an ass's head, who becomes the object of Titania's enchanted infatuation. Unity of action is triumphantly achieved.

In the content of his play Shakespeare distinguishes very clearly between two distinct planes of reality. One is the world of Theseus's Athens, a world of reason and reality even amidst the preparations for a wedding. This is the world of the bridegroom who admits to his betrothed: 'I wooed thee with my sword, / and won thy love, doing thee injuries'. It is the cruel world in which a young maiden who rejects her father's choice of a husband for her may be put to death. By way of contrast, we have the enchanted world of the woods outside Athens on a midsummer night. Here Oberon is king; here his powerful fairy magic reigns supreme and determines the destinies of those who fall within his power. And magic, like love, overthrows all reason. Indeed the magic lotion with which Oberon and Puck annoint the eyes of Titania and the human lovers symbolises the enchanting and irrational powers of love's excesses. Lysander falls out of love with Hermia and in love with Helena just as suddenly and with as little reason as Demetrius, before the opening of the play, had fallen out of love with Helena and in love with Hermia. Within the enchanted wood, as outside it, it is the men who are changeable in their affections; it is to *their* eyes that the lotion is applied. And among women, within the wood, as outside it, rivalry in love undermines true friendship. Helena is prepared to betray the confidence of her childhood friend in order to win the doubtful pleasure of Demetrius's company while he pursues the eloping Hermia and Lysander; and so, in the enchanted woods, the two friends are prepared to taunt each other and scratch each other's eyes out as they tussle to win their mates. No wonder that Puck caustically comments: 'Lord, what fools these mortals be!'

But it is not only mortals who fall victim to love's irrationalities and excesses. Titania, the fairy queen, is enamoured of an ass. Awaking to the sound of Bottom singing to keep his courage up, Titania ecstatically expresses her sudden infatuation:

> I pray thee, gentle mortal, sing again:
> Mine ear is much enamour'd of thy note;
> So is mine eye enthralled to thy shape;
> And thy fair virtue's force perforce doth move me
> On the first view to say, to swear, I love thee.
>
> (Act III, Sc. 1, 140)

Bottom's comment, despite his ass's head, is one of cold, prosaic common-sense:

> Methinks, mistress, you should have little reason for that: and yet, to say the truth, reason and love keep little company together now-a-days; the more the pity that some honest neighbours will not make them friends. . .
>
> (Act III, Sc. 1, 145)

Through the farcical events of the night in the enchanted woods of Athens, then, romantic love with its idiosyncracies and excesses is mocked and satirized. And this mockery of love continues even when we return to daylight and the rational realism of Theseus's Athens. The two couples who have emerged from their adventures in the woods are married, together with Theseus and Hippolyta, and the play chosen to be performed at the opening of the three-fold wedding celebrations is the tragedy of the ill-fated love of a pair of star-crossed lovers of ancient time, Pyramus and Thisbe.

But in the hands of the clumsy artisans who act the play, and also in the hands of the equally clumsy dramatist who must be supposed to have composed it for them, the tragedy turns into violent farce. The ridiculous doggerel-verse, the excessive use of verbal repetition and of poetic devices such as alliteration, combine with the workmen's amateurish histrionic powers to rouse the laughter and mocking comment of the royalty and aristocracy who constitute the audience of this 'play-within-a play'. In much the same way, some of the plays being performed in Shakespeare's day must have aroused the more sophisticated members of the audience to express *their* sarcasm and displeasure.

But this device of a further plane of reality in Shakespeare's play – i.e. the plane of reality of the play that is being performed before Duke Theseus in the play that is being performed before the real-life Elizabethan bridal pair — enables the author to make some very interesting comment on artistic creation in general and the art of the drama in particular. For the humour of the artisan-theme springs not only from the badness of the play they present and their manner of presenting it, but also – primarily – from the artisans' attitude to drama. Indeed it is this attitude that is the source of their manner of presentation. For the artisans are incapable of distinguishing between art and reality. Themselves lacking both in imagination and in the capacity for achieving a 'willing suspension of disbelief', they assume a similar lack in their audience. The ladies will be frightened by the lion who must therefore explain that he is in reality Snug the joiner; the moonlight must be visibly presented – in the form of the legendary man in the moon, complete with lantern, thornbush and dog; and the wall dividing the two lovers must be impersonated by Snout with loam, roughcast and stone. In short, no allowance is made, nor scope given, for the imaginative participation of the spectators. In the naïve artisans, then, Shakespeare presents the opinions of those of his contemporaries who viewed the drama as something wholly realistic and true to life. This is the attitude satirized in Beaumont and Fletcher's play *The Knight of the Burning Pestle* as the opinion of the unsophisticated, naïve middle-class audiences. It was also the attitude of those who condemned drama – as the Puritans frequently did – on the grounds that it was a form of counterfeiting calculated to mislead the conscience and undermine the morality of the audience.

However, in the figure of Theseus Shakespeare presents what is perhaps the opposite extreme: Theseus rejects drama because it is so remote from reality and reason. In his opinion even 'the best in this kind [i.e. the best of actors] are but shadows,' things of no substance. Theseus, is, in fact, always sceptical about the creations of the imagination and so we find him classing the poet together with the lunatic and the lover, when he dismisses the stories the lovers have told of their night's adventures as utter nonsense:

> Lovers and madmen have such seething brains,
> Such shaping fantasies, that apprehend
> More than cool reason ever comprehends.
> The lunatic, the lover and the poet
> Are of imagination all compact:
> One sees more devils than vast hell can hold,
> That is, the madman: the lover, all as frantic,
> Sees Helen's beauty in a brow of Egypt:
> The poet's eye, in a fine frenzy rolling,
> Doth glance from heaven to earth, from earth to heaven;
> And as imagination bodies forth
> The forms of things unknown, the poet's pen
> Turns them to shapes and gives to airy nothing
> A local habitation and a name.
> Such tricks hath strong imagination,
> That, if it would but apprehend some joy,
> It comprehends some bringer of that joy;

> Or in the night, imagining some fear,
> How easy is a bush supposed a bear!
>
> (Act V, Sc. 1, 4)

Hippolyta's demurrence to his sweeping condemnation is important:

> But all the story of the night told over,
> And all their minds transfigured so together,
> More witnesseth than fancy's images
> And grows to something of great constancy;
> But, howsoever, strange and admirable.
>
> (Act V, Sc. 1, 23)

It is the *shaping* of what the imagination has conceived, the 'telling-over' of 'fancy's images', that makes credible what is strange and marvellous. In other words, the poet's art ensures that we willingly suspend our disbelief and, for a while at least, accept as reality something that our reason perceives to be impossible. Thus, when Theseus comments on drama that 'imagination' must 'amend' the 'shadows', Hippolyta correctly adds 'It must be your imagination, then'. 'Eke out our imperfections with your minds', the chorus in *Henry V* pleads of his audience. For the drama demands an imaginative effort of its audience as well as its author, and this is borne out by the manner in which Shakespeare ended the play that his company presented at that noble marriage feast.

For it is not with the 'framework' of Theseus's daylight world of Athenian reason and rationalism that Shakespeare rounded off his play, as dramatic logic perhaps demanded. Suddenly the doubly make-believe world of Athens's fairies fuses with the reality of the Elizabethan audience. Oberon and Titania and their fairy train step foward to pronounce a benediction over 'this hallowed house' – and it is not only the stage fabric of Theseus's palace but also the Elizabethan mansion that they refer to. When they dance off to bless the 'best bridebed' and frolick through 'each several chamber' of 'this palace', the fairies step off the stage to take their way out through the audience, as the actors in the Elizabethan mask traditionally mingled with the audience at the end of the entertainment.

Dream and reality are, by the great artist, fused and blended together indistinguishably. Awakening in the woods, the four Athenian lovers, as also Titania and Bottom, had thought the fantastic events of the night to be a dream. But in fact we, the audience, know that the events *did* take place, through the magic powers of Oberon. And the after-effects of those events are apparent even after the awakening: Demetrius now returns Helena's love and Oberon retains the Indian boy whom Titania had relinquished to him while she was under the influence of the magic spell. All is not now as it had been before.

And, just as dream and reality are fused within the framework of the play itself, so now Puck – or rather the actor who has been playing Puck – steps forward out of the make-believe stage world to address us, Shakespeare's audience, directly:

> If we *shadows* have offended,
> Think but this, and all is mended,
> That you have but slumber'd here
> While these visions did appear.
> And this weak and idle theme,
> No more yielding but a dream,
> Gentles, do not reprehend:
>
> (Act V, Sc. 1, 430)

The analogy is clear and it is underlined by the fact that 'Puck' applies to himself and the play in which he has appeared the same term that Theseus - and, indeed, the Elizabethans in general – applied to all actors: 'shadows'. As Oberon with his magic created a reality which, to those caught up in it, had all the qualities of a dream and a vision, so Shakespeare the poet with *his* magic art has temporarily created a reality out of what, rationally, we perceive to be visions, dreams, creatures of the imagination, shadows rather than substance.

Behind the apparent humility of the apologia-epilogue lies the actual pride of actor and dramatist (and we must remember that Shakespeare was both) in their profession. For patently Shakespeare's verse and dramatic power, unlike the horrid doggerel of *Pyramus and Thisbe*, have succeeded in achieving the willing suspension of our disbelief. By a joint act of the imagination on the part of author and audience magic has been temporarily transformed into reality and reality transfused with the golden glow of magic.

By Alice Shalvi

The Element of Imagination in *A Midsummer Night's Dream*

A Midsummer Night's Dream is one of the lightest and in many respects the most purely playful of Shakespeare's plays. Yet it is surpassed by few if any of his early works in its importance for an understanding of the unfolding of his genius. It is characteristic of its author that he should have chosen this fanciful dream-play through which to announce for the first time in overt and unmistakable fashion the conviction that underlies every one of his supreme Tragedies: that this world of sense in which we live is but the surface of a vaster unseen world by which the actions of men are affected or overruled. He had already in *The Comedy of Errors* hinted at a witchcraft at work behind events. But that at the moment seemed little more than the author's apology for the amount of coincidence in his plot. Now he begins to explore the causes of coincidence. Not until the end of his career, in *The Tempest,* was he to treat this theme with such directness, not even in *Macbeth*. It may be objected that this is taking a mere dream or fantasy quite too seriously. It is of course possible to hold that in *A Midsummer Night's Dream* Shakespeare is not so much giving utterance to convictions of his own as recording a folklore which itself carries certain metaphysical implications. There is doubtless some truth in this view – how much it is hard to tell. But it makes little difference. For the implications, in the latter case, were the seeds of the convictions, and our mistake, if any, is merely that of finding the oak in the acorn. The congruity, in spite of their differences, of *A Midsummer Night's Dream* with *The Tempest* is one of the most striking demonstrations of the continuity and integrity of Shakespeare's genius that his works afford.

There are two passages, as distinct from incidents, in *A Midsummer Night's Dream* that perhaps above all others embody its central theme. Each enhances the other. One of them, Theseus' well-known speech on the imagination at the beginning of Act V, has always been accorded due importance. The other, oddly, though almost as universally praised, has generally been looked on as a kind of digression, a purple patch that justifies itself by its own beauty rather than through any particular pertinence to the rest of the play. The lines have been widely and deservedly acclaimed for their sound. But their euphony is only one aspect of their miraculous quality. The passage is the one in the first scene of Act IV where Theseus and Hippolyta, just as the dogs are about to be released for the hunt, speak of the music of the hounds in words that by some magic catch and echo that very music itself:

THE.: My love shall hear the music of my hounds.
　　　Uncoupled in the western valley; let them go:
　　　Dispatch, I say, and find the forester.
　　　We will, fair queen, up to the mountain's top,
　　　And mark the musical confusion
　　　Of hounds and echo in conjunction.
HIP.: I was with Hercules and Cadmus once,
　　　When in a wood of Crete they bay'd the bear
　　　With hounds of Sparta: never did I hear
　　　Such gallant chiding; for, besides the groves,
　　　The skies, the fountains, every region near
　　　Seem'd all one mutual cry. I never heard
　　　So musical a discord, such sweet thunder.
THE.: My hounds are bred out of the Spartan kind,
　　　So flew'd, so sanded; and their heads are hung
　　　With ears that sweep away the morning dew;
　　　Crook-knee'd, and dew-lapp'd like Thessalian bulls;
　　　Slow in pursuit, but match'd in mouth like bells,
　　　Each under each. A cry more tuneable
　　　Was never holla'd to, nor cheer'd with horn,

In Crete, in Sparta, nor in Thessaly:
Judge, when you hear.

This a digression! On the contrary it is as nearly perfect a metaphor as could be conceived for *A Midsummer Night's Dream* itself and for the incomparable counterpoint with which its own confusions and discords are melted into the "sweet thunder" of a single musical effect. How can British fairies and Athenian nobility be mingled with decency in the same play? As easily as the "confusion" of hounds and echoes can make "conjunction." How can the crossings and bewilderments of the four lovers lead to their happy reunion at the end? As easily as discord can contribute to harmony in music. How can the foolish and awkward pranks of the rustics adorn the wedding celebration of a great duke? As easily, to turn things the other way around, as a fairy dream can enter the head of an ass or as animals who are like bulls can emit sounds that are like bells – as easily as thunder can be sweet.

The very incongruities, anachronisms, contradictions, and impossible juxtapositions of *A Midsummer Night's Dream,* and the triumphant manner in which the poet reduces them to a harmony, are what more than anything else make this play a masterpiece. The hounds are symbols of the hunt, and so of death. But their voices are transmuted by distance, in the ear of the listener, to symbols of harmony and life. The hunt is called off; the will of the cruel father is overborne; a triple wedding is substituted for it:

Our purpos'd hunting shall be set aside.
Away with us to Athens: three and three,
We'll hold a feast in great solemnity.

We might discover the whole history of humanity, past and future, in those lines.

It is right here that the passage about the hounds links with Theseus' speech on the imagination. The Duke, in words too well known to need quotation, tells of the power of this faculty, whether in the lunatic, the lover, or the poet, to create something out of nothing. The poet alone, however, has power to capture this "airy nothing" and anchor it, as it were, to reality, even as Shakespeare gives actuality to fairies in this very play. Yet Theseus is suspicious of the "tricks" of imagination, conscious of its illusory quality. He hints that it must be brought to the test of "cool reason." Strictly, what Theseus is talking about is not imagination at all in its proper sense, but fantasy. Hippolyta catches just this distinction and for once seems wiser than her lover. She holds that the mircles of love are even greater than those of fancy, and because the same mircle takes place at the same time in more than one mind she believes that they testify to something solid and lasting that emerges from this "airy nothing." Theseus had called this faculty more strange than true. Hippolyta holds it both strange and true:

But all the story of the night told over,

> And all their minds transfigur'd so together,
> More witnesseth than fancy's images,
> And grows to something of great constancy,
> But, howsoever, strange and admirable.

In practice Theseus agrees with this exactly, as is shown later in the same scene when he insists on hearing the play that the craftsmen have prepared. The master of revels, Philostrate, protests against is selection:

PHIL.:   in all the play
  There is not one word apt, one player fitted.
    . . . No, my noble lord,
  It is not for you. I have heard it over,
  And it is nothing, nothing in the world. . . .
THE.:   I will hear that play;
  For never anything can be amiss,
  When simpleness and duty tender it. . . .
HIP.: He says they can do nothing in this kind.
THE.: The kinder we, to give them thanks for nothing.

That four-times reiterated "nothing" is Shakespeare's way of sending our minds back to the "airy nothing" of Theseus' earlier speech which, he then said and now proves, imagination has power to turn into something actual. It is Hippolyta this time who fails.

> This is the silliest stuff that ever I heard,*

she protests as the play proceeds. Appropriately, now that it is a question of art, Theseus turns out to be wiser than she, as she was wiser than he when it was a question of love. "The best in this kind are but shadows," he reminds her, "and the worst are not worse, if imagination amend them." At last, Theseus is using "imagination" in its proper sense, and in his words we seem to catch the very accent and secret of the poet's own tolerance and sympathy.

Shakespeare, in this play and elsewhere, was only too well aware how frail imagination can appear in the face of ineluctable fact. "The course of true love never did run smooth." "So quick bright things come to confusion."

> These things seem small and undistinguishable,
> Like far-off mountains turned into clouds.

What, indeed, is more insubstantial than a midsummer night's dream? And yet from about this time, if not from the beginning, he never lost faith in "bright things," in the power of the imagination to transmute the lead of life into its own gold. More and more, if with some ebbings, some descents into

---

*Just what Samuel Pepys said of *A Midsummer Night's Dream* itself, "The most insipid ridiculous play that ever I saw."

the valleys, this faith grew in him, in Hippolyta's words, to "something of great constancy." Is it any wonder, after the miracle that Imagination had performed through him in this very play?

A Midsummer Night's Dream is a kind of fugue with four voices

> match'd in mouth like bells,
> Each under each.

There are the fairies. There are the lovers. There are the rustics. There is the court. What metaphysical as well as social gulfs divide them! But Imagination bridges them all. Imagination makes them all one.

And the play has four voices in another and profounder sense.

A Midsummer Night's Dream is itself, as its title says, a dream. Its action occurs mostly at night. Its atmosphere is that of moonlight and shadows. Its characters are forever falling asleep and dreaming. And at the end Puck invites the audience to believe that as they have been sitting there they have nodded and slumbered and that all that has passed before them has been a vision.

But as the other part of its title suggests, *A Midsummer Night's Dream* is not only a dream, it is "play" in the quite literal sense of that term, a piece pervaded with the atmosphere of innocent idleness and joy befitting a mid-summer night. It is not merely a play; it is the spirit of play in its essence. From the pranks of Puck and the frolics of the fairies, through the hide-and-seek of the lovers in the wood and the rehearsals of the rustics, on to the wedding festivities of the court and the final presentation of the masque of Pyramus and Thisbe, the tone of the piece is that of love-in-idleness, of activity for the sheer fun of it and for its own sake.

And because *A Midsummer Night's Dream* is permeated with this spirit of doing things just for the love of doing them or for the love of the one for whom they are done, because the drama opens and closes on the wedding note and what comes between is just an interweaving of love stories, the piece may be said to be not only *dream* from end to end, and *play* from end to end, but also *love* from end to end.

And finally *A Midsummer Night's Dream* is *art* from end to end – not just a work of art itself, which of course it is, but dedicated in good measure to the theme of art and made up of many little works of art of varying degrees of merit: its innumerable songs, its perpetual references to music, its rehearsal and presentation of the story of Pyramus and Thisbe, to say nothing of its many quotable passages, which, like the one about the hounds, the one about the superiority of silence to eloquence, the one about true love, the one about the mermaid on the dolphin's back, when lifted from their context seem like poems or pictures complete in themselves, whatever subtle values they may have in relation to the whole.

Dream, play, love, art. Surely it is no coincidence that these four "subjects" which are here interwoven with such consummate polyphony represent the four main aspects under which Imagination reveals itself in human life. Dream: what is that but a name for the world out of which man emerges into conscious life, the world of the unconscious as we have a habit of calling it today? Play: the instrument by which the child instinctively repeats the experience of the race and so by rehearsal prepares himself for the drama of life. Love: a revelation to each of the sexes that it is but a fragment of Another, which, by combined truth and illusion, seems at first concentrated in a person of the opposite sex. Art: the dream become conscious of itself, play grown to an adult estate, love freed of its illusion and transferred to wider and higher than personal ends. Dream, play, love, art: these four. Is there a fifth?

The fifth perhaps is what we finally have in this play, a union of the other four, Imagination in its quintessence – not just dream, nor play, nor love, nor art, but something above and beyond them all. With the attainment of it, the first becomes last, dream comes full circle as Vision, an immediate conscious apprehension of an invisible world, or, if you will, transubstantiation of the world of sense into something beyond itself. *

The example of Bottom and his transformation will serve to bring these un-Shakespearean abstractions back to the concrete. To the average reader, Puck and Bottom are probably the most memorable characters in the play, Bottom especially. This instinct is right. Bottom is as much the master-character here as Launce is in *The Two Gentlemen of Verona*. Bottom symbolizes the earthy, the ponderous, the slow, in contrast with Puck, who is all that is quick, light, and aerial. Bottom is substance, the real in the common acceptation of that term. If Puck is the apex, Bottom is the base without whose four-square foundation the pyramid of life would topple over. He is the antithesis of the thesis of the play, the ballast that keeps the elfin bark of it from capsizing. He is literally what goes to the bottom. Like all heavy things he is content with his place in life, but his egotism is the unconscious selfishness of a child, both a sense and a consequence of his own individuality, not greed but pride in the good significance of that word. His realistic conception of stagecraft is in character. To Puck, Bottom is an ass. Yet Titania falls in love with him, ass's head and all.

> And I will purge thy mortal grossness so
> That though shalt like an airy spirit go,

she promises. And she keeps her promise by sending him Bottom's dream.

The moment when Bottom awakens from this dream is the supreme moment of the play.† There is nothing more wonderful in the poet's early

---

*I refrain from using the word Religion for this ultimate phase of the Imagination. A word so contaminated with theological, ecclesiastic, and moral considerations can lead only to confusion. If the word were only uncontaminated, it might be a near synonym for Vision as I use it.

†"I have had a most rare vision. I have had a dream, past the wit of man to say what dream it was. Man is but an ass, if he go about to expound this dream. Methought I was – there is no man can tell what. Methought I was, – and methought I had, – but man is but a patch'd fool, if he will offer to say what methought I had. The eye of man hath not heard, the ear of man hath not seen, man's hand is not able to taste, his tongue to conceive, nor his heart to report, what my dream was. I will get Peter Quince to write a ballad of this dream. It shall be called 'Bottom's Dream,' because it hath no bottom; and I will sing it in the latter end of a play, before the Duke; peradventure, to make it the more gracious, I shall sing it at her death."

works and few things more wonderful in any of them. For what Shakespeare has caught here in perfection is the original miracle of Imagination, the awakening of spiritual life in the animal man. Bottom is an ass. If Bottom can be redeemed, matter itself and man in all his materiality can be redeemed also. Democracy becomes possible. Nothing less than this is what this incident implies. Yet when it is acted, so far as my experience in the theater goes, this divine insight is reduced to nothing but an occasion for roars of laughter. Laughter of course there should be, but laughter shot through with a beauty and pathos close to tears. Only an actor of genius could do justice to it. Bottom himself best indicates its quality when he declares that the dream deserves to be *sung* at the conclusion of a play and that it should be called Bottom's dream "because it hath no bottom." It is the same thought that Thoreau expounds when he shows why men persist in believing in bottomless ponds. For a moment in this scene, however far over the horizon, we sense the Shakespeare who was to describe the death of Falstaff, compose *King Lear,* and create Caliban.

Indeed, *A Midsummer Night's Dream* as a whole is prophetic, in one respect at least, as is no other of the earlier plays, of the course the poet's genius was to take. There are few more fruitful ways of regarding his works than to think of them as an account of the warfare between Imagination and Chaos – or, if you will, between Imagination and the World – the story of the multifarious attempts of the divine faculty in man to ignore, to escape, to outwit, to surmount, to combat, to subdue, to forgive, to convert, to redeem, to transmute into its own substance, as the case may be, the powers of disorder that possess the world. Taken retrospectively, *A Midsummer Night's Dream* seems like the argument of this story, like an overture to the vast musical composition which the poet's later masterpieces make up, like a seed from which the Shakespearean flower developed and unfolded.

By Harold C. Goddard

The Supernatural In
A Midsummer Night's Dream

. . . A study of Shakespeare and the Supernatural follows the Poet through his changing moods, and throws a new light upon the process of his development which enables us to understand him better. In *Midsummer Night's Dream* we deal with the Shakespeare of the first period – the period of the early comedies and the Chronicle Plays. He is young enough still to retain more than glimpses of that light-hearted, observant, and interested boy who walked the lanes and fields of Stratford. He has not been in London so long, he has not become so engrossed in erudite scholarship, that the woodland notes and the song of the river are not still clearly audible to him. A happy optimism remains the trend of his active mind. This coloured everything he handled and is nowhere more evident than in his first dramatic use of the Supernatural.

The form of the Supernatural employed by the Poet in *Midsummer Night's Dream* is fairies. Fairies gave him a full opportunity to follow his bent and allow free rein to his imagination. He revels in imagery. He reveals himself in the following lines (Act V, Sc. 1, 12-17):

> The poet's eye, in a fine frenzy rolling,
> Doth glance from heaven to earth, from earth to heaven;
> And, as imagination bodies forth
> The forms of things unknown, the poet's pen
> Turns them to shapes, and gives to airy nothing
> A local habitation and a name.

Shakespeare's choice of Fairies was, however, not dictated solely by his own feelings and preference as a poet. Obviously he welcomed the suggestion and was thoroughly happy in working it out, but most probably it had another origin than his own fertile brain. *Midsummer Night's Dream* was written to be performed at a wedding. There cannot be much doubt about that. The plot itself makes it quite clear. As to whose wedding Shakespeare intended to honour there is less certainty. Several have been put forward and supported by ingenious argument; but the occasion that appeals to us most is the marriage of the Poet's patron, the Earl of Southampton, to Mistress Elizabeth Vernon. The objection is that this happy event did not take place until 1598, while it is beyond doubt that he was at work on the play before this. *A* wedding rather than *whose* wedding is the point that concerns us at the moment; for the Elizabethans associated Fairies very intimately with these functions, and so naturally determined the dramatist's choice of this form of the Supernatural.

None was more qualified to handle a fairy theme successfully than the young poet of the Warwickshire countryside, who knew all the rustic beliefs about these little people and was once upon a time a firm believer himself in their existence. The scholastic product of the university, steeped in classical lore and hedged in by science and philosophy, could not easily escape into the fantastic realm of fairyland and give a convincing picture of its life and people. For Shakespeare this presented no difficulties.

Those who deny the poet the ability to originate a plot, and take a delight in tracing every incident of his stories to some source or other, are in difficulties with *Midsummer Night's Dream*. Apart from current fairy-lore, with which he became familiar enough in his childhood, the play seems to be almost wholly the creation of the Poet's own fancy. In the other fairy play, *The Tempest*, the critics are again compelled to give Shakespeare the credit for thinking out the plot for himself; while *Macbeth*, though he obtained a hint for the Weird Sisters from Holinshed, the whole conception of the witch character is entirely unlike that of any other man. In the Supernatural, therefore, we find the Poet's creative faculty at its busiest.

Shakespeare's use of the Fairies is original and clever. He avoids anything heavy. He deserts the unattractive fancies of folk-lore for delightful beings of his own creation. He does not employ the Supernatural in this early play with any special dramatic purpose beyond the desire to entertain. He does not attach any particular meaning or significance to his Little People, nor does he endow them with any great powers or control over mortals. Undoubtedly he shows considerable ingenuity in his dramatic construction by deftly interweaving the three themes – the quarrels of the lovers, the fooling of Bottom and the clowns, and the meddling interference of the Fairies. As a whole, though, he writes in happy, carefree vein, drawing prodigally on his imagination, and adopting the attitude of one who has made startling discoveries of the truth about fairies and has decided to pass his knowledge on to his fellows.

There is the spontaneity of effortless creation in Shakespeare's handling of the Fairies of the *Dream*. He does not keep his light and aery beings separate from his mortal characters, as the Weird Sisters are kept separate in *Macbeth*. The Fairies mix freely with the very worldly men and women of the Court of Theseus; and, be it noted, in these scenes it is the human element that is dominant, whereas the enchanted forest is the kingdom where the Fairies have their own way without effective opposition. The Poet, however, does not in this early incursion into the realm of the Supernatural endow his immortals with any real influence over the human soul. Certainly they are guilty of much mischievous interference, which causes a good deal of temporary annoyance, but there is no evidence of any power to tempt, to deceive with malice, or to destroy.

When Shakespeare resolved to enter fairyland, he was not content with any half-way house. He reached the very heart of Oberon and Titania's kingdom. He clothed his Fairies in many of the common superstititions which he had gathered from years of sojourn amongst convinced believers. Few of the rustics of the Stratford country would care to deny the existence of the Little People. They were too frightened of being paid out for their disloyalty by some mischievous prank on the part of a local fay. But Shakespeare's Fairies differed greatly from the products of rustic belief. Mr. Harry Furness writes: "The fairies of folk-lore were rough and repulsive, taking their style from the hempen homespuns who invented them." In *The Elizabethan Fairies* Mr. M. W. Latham explains at length how utterly unlike the troublesome folk-fairies were the delightful beings of Shakespeare. Titania, Oberon, and their trains, are fairies of "another sort"; and Shakespeare undoubtedly owed a great deal in their conception to the old Greek writers. We can recognize in them "the nymphs and fauns, the naiads and dryads of Greece."[1] There he found the grace and beauty of his Titania and her subjects. But, as usual, he was not content to copy. He did not merely reproduce the Nymphs, Fauns, and Satyrs of mythology. He draped their forms artistically in current superstitions, softening their classical character, and making them thoroughly English and modern.

The little band of *Midsummer Night's Dream* are to be understood as

1. *The Supernatural in Shakespeare*, Helen H. Stewart, p. 97.

diminutive in size, for we learn that, while Titania and Oberon are quarrelling over the changeling boy, their subject-elves "for fear Creep into acorn cups and hide them there" (Act II, Sc. 1, 30-31). Again, we have Titania's commands to her subjects at the beginning of Act II, Scene 2:

> Come, now a roundel and a fairy song;
> Then, for the third part of a minute, hence;
> Some to kill cankers in the musk-rose buds;
> Some war with rere-mice for their leathern wings
> T make my small elves coats; and some keep back
> The clamorous owl, that nightly hoots and wonders
> At our quaint spirits.

The matter of size was one of Shakespeare's principal departures from popular ideas, which pictured the folk-fairies as equal in stature to smally made mortals.

The immortality of the Fairies is made clear from several passages. Puck remarks contemptuously of the humans, "Lord, what fools these mortals be!" (Act III, Sc. 2, 115); and Titania, speaking of the mother of her Indian protégé, says (Act II, Sc. 1, 135-137):

> But she, being mortal, of that boy did die;
> And for her sake do I rear up her boy;
> And for her sake I will not part with him.

When waking beneath Oberon's spell Titania falls instantly in love with the ass-pated Bottom, addresses hims as "gentle mortal," and promises: "I will purge thy mortal grossness" (Act III, Sc. 1, 163). When she is released from her spell by the Fairy King, she inquires of him how it came about that she was found sleeping with mortals on the ground (Act IV, Sc. 1, 104-107).

Further evidence of immortality lies in the strange powers which the Fairies are shown to possess. These powers were all drawn from popular superstition. Firstly, there is the ability to make themselves invisible. Oberon finds this useful when Demetrius appears in the wood with Helena following him. He says (Act II, Sc. 1, 186-187):

> But who comes here? I am invisible;
> And I will overhear their conference.

Puck takes full advantage of his invisibility when he plays his cruel joke on Bottom; and he and Oberon are able to listen-in to the confusion amongst the lovers without risk of detection.

Not only were fairies thought to be able to vanish at will, but they enjoyed great powers of metamorphosis and could assume almost any shape they pleased. Puck glories in the opportunities for mischief which this gives him. He says to the Fairy (Act II, Sc. 1, 43-48):

I am that merry wanderer of the night.
I jest to Oberon, and make him smile,
When I a fat and bean-fed horse beguile,
Neighing in likeness of a filly foal:
And sometime lurk I in a gossip's bowl,
In very likeness of a roasted crab.

Again, he calls after Quince and his friends (Act III, Sc. 1, 109-114):

I'll follow you, I'll lead you about a round,
Through bog, through bush, through brake, through brier:
Sometime a horse I'll be, sometime a hound,
A hog, a headless bear, sometime a fire;
And neigh, and bark, and grunt, and roar, and burn,
Like horse, hound, hog, bear, fire, at every turn.

The speed with which the Fairies move shows that they are not fettered by mortal limitations of time and space. Puck says that he goes "swifter than arrow from the Tarter's bow" (Act III, Sc. 2, 101) and boasts that he can "put a girdle round about the earth in forty minutes" (Act II, Sc. 1, 175-176). One of Titania's fairies tells Puck (Act II, Sc. 1, 6-7):

I do wander everywhere,
Swifter than the moon's sphere.

Fairies exercised considerable influence over weather conditions and in a measure were able to control them. Titania tells Oberon that the quarrel between tham has had most disastrous climatic results:

. . . the winds . . .
. . . have suck'd up from the sea
Contagious fogs; which, falling in the land,
Have every pelting river made so proud,
That they have overborne their continents.
(Act II, Sc. 1, 88-92.)

After listing a number of other disasters, she continues (*ibid.*, 107-117):

The seasons alter: hoary-headed frosts
Fall in the fresh lap of the crimson rose;
And on old Hiem's thin and icy crown
An odorous chaplet of sweet summer buds
Is, as in mockery, set: the spring, the summer,
The chiding autumn, angry winter, change
Their wonted liveries, and the mazed world,
By their increase, now knows not which is which:
And this same progeny of evils comes

From our debate, from our dissension;
We are their parents and original.

In the above exquisite lines the Poet suggests that chaotic conditions must follow quarrels among the Fairies, whose duty it is to order them. Oberon's power over the elements is illustrated in Act II, Scene 2, when, seeing that Lysander and Demetrius are bent on a fight, he commands Puck (355-359):

Hie, therefore, Robin, overcast the night;
The starry welkin cover thou anon
With drooping fog, as black as Acheron;
And lead these testy rivals so astray,
As one comes not within another's way.

Fancy gave the Fairies the most beautiful dwelling places:

. . .in dale, forest, or mead,
By paved fountain or by rushy brook,
Or in the beached margent of the sea.

(Act II, Sc. 1, 83-85.)

And what could be more lovely than Titania's couch?

. . . a bank where the wild thyme blows,
Where oxlips and the nodding violet grows;
Quite over-canopied with luscious woodbine,
With sweet must-roses, and with eglantine.

(*ibid.*, 249-252.)

The soft, scented summer night, under the gentle light of the argent moon, was the time the Fairies chose for their fun and frolic. Says Theseus in the last scene of the play, "The iron tongue of midnight hath told twelve: . . . 'tis almost fairy time" (Act V, Sc. 1, 370-371). By the time dawn broke fairies should be safe in their haunts. When Oberon explains to Puck all he means to do to straighten out the tangles, which are mostly of the imp's making, he receives the answer (Act III, Sc. 2, 378-380):

My fairy lord, this must be done with haste,
For night's swift dragons cut the clouds full fast,
And yonder shines Aurora's harbinger.

Puck is a conventional sprite in so far that he thinks it improper, even dangerous, for any of his tribe to be abroad in daylight. Oberon boasts that he has lingered in the forest until the sun has actually risen. But he seems to regard these occasions as exceptionally daring, and tells Puck that, if they do not delay, "We may effect this business yet ere day" (Act III, Sc. 2, 394). As the title of the play suggests, it is the warm nights of June that the Fairies enjoy. Titania says, "The summer still doth tend upon my state" (Act III, Sc. 1, 158). When winter comes, they migrate like the swallows to warmer lands, such as "the spiced Indian air" (Act II, Sc. 1, 124).

Immortal though they may be, the Fairies partake of mortal pleasures. They eat, drink, and make merry, and are particularly fond of music and dancing. Titania complains bitterly to Oberon that his brawls have disturbed their sport when they have met to dance their ringlets to the whistling wind (Act II, Sc. 1, 86-87). The "ringlets" are a reference to those circles of bright-green grass, which were then supposed to be made by the Fairies, but which science has now coldly explained to be a growth of fungi. Another mention of the fairy rings occurs in Act II, Scene 1, where the Fairy tells Puck:

> And I serve the fairy queen,
> To dew her orbs upon the green.

The main characteristic of the Fairies of *Midsummer Night's Dream* is their penchant for mischief. They are always meddling and interfering in other people's affairs, especially Puck, who is the very embodiment of rascality. There is, however, no malice in their fun. They are just naughty children, naturally happy, laughing and skipping about, easily frightened, and repentant when scolded. They do not hate. When a joke has gone too far, they are ready and willing to put matters right again. Oberon clears up the muddle which Puck has made in anointing Lysander, and not Demetrius, with the love-potion, and releases Titania from her infatuation for Bottom. Goodwill is expressed in Puck's speech at the end of Act III, when curing Lysander:

> Jack shall have Jill;
> Nought shall go ill;

> The man shall have his mare again, and all shall be well.

And again, at the end of the play:

> Give me your hands, if we be friends,
> And Robin shall restore amends.

Original though his own conception of the Fairies is, Shakespeare packs *Midsummer Night's Dream* with folk-lore and popular fairy beliefs. To the many already noted we must add the changeling boy. Abduction of human beings was among the Fairies' chief activities, though the motive is obscure. Shakespeare's more refined conception improves upon the general version. Titania has robbed no human cradle, but has brought up the child for the sake of friendship with the mother, who, "being mortal, of that boy did die" (Act II, Sc. 1, 135). Changelings, as a rule, caused much heartache and anxiety.

An important and delightful feature of the fantasy is the fairy music which is interspersed throughout. . . .

At the end of Elizabeth's reign the English could be described with some justice as a musical nation. Music held an important place in the school curriculum; and those who could not read a part at sight, or play some instrument like the lute or viol, were thought to have gravely neglected an essential side of their education. Commentators have established the truth that Shakespeare was not only extremely fond of music, but also had a sound technical knowledge of it. Certainly he was fully aware of its effect and influence on theatre audiences. He used music freely when presenting the mysterious and ethereal. It was closely associated in his mind with the preternatural. As a poet he accepted the Pythagorean notion of the music of the spheres, and in the famous lines on music in *The Merchant of Venice* makes Lorenzo declare (Act V, Sc. 1, 63-65):

> Such harmony is in immortal souls;
> But while this muddy vesture of decay
> Doth grossly close it in, we cannot hear it.

In *Midsummer Night's Dream* music materially assists Shakespeare in creating that fairy atmosphere which is so enchanting, visionary, and idealistic.

Titania, we have seen, early reveals herself as a music-lover by her protest to Oberon that his brawls have disturbed the fairy dances to the piping winds (Act II, Sc. 1, 86-87). In the following scene she calls to her attendants, "Come, now a roundel and a fairy song" and later says. "Sing me now to sleep . . . and let me rest". She dozes off as the firsl Fairy sings the dainty song, "You spotted snakes", and all the other little voices join in the soothing lullaby chorus. When releasing Titania from his charm, Oberon bids her "music call"; and Titania responds with "Music, ho! music such as charmeth sleep" (Act IV, Sc. 1, 88). The king and queen then dance together to a lilting strain while the effect of the magic spell passes from the entangled lovers, Lysander, Demetrius, Hermia, and Helena. At the end of the play, when the happily married couples have retired, Oberon, Titania, and their fairy train, led by Puck, creep in by the "glimmering light" of the "drowsy fire," and skipping through the sleeping house, with song and dance pour out a blessing on the newly wed. Though not marked in the Stage Directions, the final passage (from line 398) is usually sung, the lines commencing "Now, until the break of day" being one of the few Shakespearean dance-songs. Similarly, the Fairy's speech, "Over hill, over dale" (Act II, Sc. 1, 2-13), is treated as a song; while "I know a bank where the wild thyme blows" (Act II, Sc. 1, 249 *et seq.)* is frequently made into a solo for Oberon. Apart from Bottom's outburst into a frankly rural ditty, the music of *Midsummer Night's Dream* is in keeping with the immortal and fantastic theme, and gives that airy, gossamer-like effect, which was wonderfully recaptured by the genius of Mendelssohn.

Puck, the sprightly messenger of Oberon and Titania, embodies practically everything that tradition said about the fairy love of mischief-making. Puck is strictly speaking the title for a class of malicious, teasing sprites; and the name of Oberon's court jester is more properly Robin Goodfellow, the popular practical joker of folk-lore. The Fairies hardly regarded Puck as one of themselves, for he was bigger than they and was more of the brownie.[1] The dialogue between him and the Fairy, which opens Act II, gives the keynote of the whole play. First the fairy describes her night's duties as a subject of

---

1. II. Littledale in *Shakespeare's England*, I. 539.

Titania, and then Puck speaks of Oberon's revels and warns the Fairy of his master's resentment against her mistress over her refusal to let him have the Indian boy as a page. The Fairy then recognizes the brownie (Act II, Sc. 1, 32-34):

> Either I mistake your shape and making quite,
> Or else you are that shrewd and knavish sprite
> Call'd Robin Goodfellow: are not you he
> That frights the maidens of the villagery;
> Skim milk, and sometimes labour in the quern,
> And bootless make the breathless housewife churn;
> And sometime make the drink to bear no barm;
> Mislead night-wanderers, laughing at their harm?
> Those that Hobgoblin call you, and sweet Puck,
> You do their work, and they shall have good luck:
> Are not you he?

Puck confesses, "I am that merry wanderer of the night," and proceeds to tell the Fairy of his jests and practical jokes. Further on in the play he admits again, "Those things do best please me, that befall preposterously" (Act III, Sc. 2, 120-121).

As H. Littledale writes in *Shakespeare's England*,[1] Puck has "nearly as many aliases as he has transformations." The names already mentioned, Robin Goodfellow and Hobgoblin, seem to be the same, for "Hob" was merely a variation for "Robert" or "Robin."[2] Another of his characters was Lob-lie-by-the-fire, a house-elf, who entered the homesteads and did menial service. He is addressed by the Fairy as "Thou lob (i.e. clown) of Spirits" (Act II, Sc. 1, 16). When he "misled night-wanderers," he was Will-o'-the-wisp, Jack-o'-lantern, or Kit-with-the-canstick, the folk-lore explanation of that phenomenon known as "ignis fatuus." He is thoroughly English in character, and is used to portray all the roguishness and rascality of the Fairies in their most mischievous mood.

Oberon, the King of the Fairies, rules a band of subjects who are the joint creations of folk-lore and mythology. His dwelling is the forest, where he indulges in feasts and revellings with a splendid court, and uses his supernatural powers for no higher end than his own amusement. He plans most of the mischief which Puck carries out, though the imp, both carelessly and intentionally, improves upon his instructions. There is no malice in Oberon, quarrelsome though he may be. He straightens out the lovers' tangle, makes it up with Titania, and gives his blessing to Theseus and his court when the triple wedding is celebrated.

An Oberon appeared on the stage before Shakespeare's immortal in Greene's *James IV*, where he is called "Oboram, King of the Fayeries." The name seems to have come originally from the Charlemagne romance, *Huon of Bordeaux*, which was translated from the French by Lord Berners about 1534.

1. I. 539.
2. M. W. Latham in *The Elizabethan Fairies* suggests that Hobgoblin was a separate spirit.

This Auberon, as the name was there spelt, was reputed to be the son of Julius Caesar and the sister of the British King Arthur, Morgan le Fay. He may be identified with the dwarf Alberich in the German epic, *Nibelungen Lied,* who dwelt with his fairy-subjects in a forest on the way to Babylon. All that part of the world was loosely known to Shakespeare's contemporaries as "India." Hence, Oberon has come to the wood near Athens "from the farthest steppe of India" (Act II, Sc. 1, 69); and it is an Indian boy over whom he quarrels with Titania. Titania clings to the changeling for love of the dead mother, who was her bosom companion "in the spiced Indian air" (Act II, Sc. 1, 124). Oberon of *Midsummer Night's Dream* is, however, entirely different to Auberon of *Huon of Bordeaux.* He is a wholly Shakespearean creation and composed of the elements of classical tradition mixed with the country superstitions which the Warwickshire Poet knew and loved.

The name Titania means "a daughter of the Titans." The Titans were the rulers of heaven and earth until overthrown by Zeus, or Jupiter, who made himself Lord of Olympus. "Titania," then, presumed a very long pedigree indeed; and the name was applied by Ovid in his *Metamorphoses* to the goddess Diana." There Shakespeare found it, and in the original Latin, too. Golding in his English translation of the *Metamorphoses* does not write the word "Titania" at all, but uses other expressions in its place. It would seem from this that Shakespeare's Latin was not so "small" as Ben Jonson would have us believe.

The grace and dignity of the classical Diana are retained in Shakespeare's Titania, though the character as a whole is a lighter and more beautiful conception. But the Poet kept the goddess in mind, for it was generally believed at the time that the nymphs who attended her were identical with the medieval Fairies. Titania queens it in a moonlit, woodland kingdom; and though she has traces of mischievousness, she is not that player of vexatious pranks who was known among country folk as Queen Mab.[1] For the quarrel between Titania and Oberon, it is probable that Shakespeare remembered Chaucer's *Merchant's Tale* and gathered a hint or two from it.

The little Fairies, Peaseblossom, Cobweb, Moth, and Mustard-seed, who are instructed by Titania to be "kind and courteous" to Bottom, are apparently the product of Shakespeare's fancy alone. Their names suggest beauties of Nature personified, and their presence gives an excuse for intro-ducing many of the quaint ideas of the countryside. Hear Titania's instructions to them (Act III, Sc. 1, 167-177):

> Be kind and courteous to this gentleman;
> Hop in his walks, and gambol in his eyes;
> Feed him with apricocks and dewberries,
> With purple grapes, green figs, and mulberries;
> The honey-bags steal from the humble bees,
> And, for night-tapers, crop their waxen thighs,

1. For Shakespeare's description of Queen Mab, see the lines in *Romeo and Juliet,* Act I, Scene 4, 55-69.

And light them at the fiery glow-worm's eyes,
To have my love to bed, and to arise;
And pluck the wings from painted butterflies,
To fan the moonbeams from his sleeping eyes:
Nod to him, elves, and do him courtesies.

Shakespeare makes no attempt in *Midsummer Night's Dream* at a serious discussion on the real existence of fairies. Whether his audience believes or disbelieves is no concern of his. For the purposes of his fantasy he writes as if there were no doubt upon the matter, but he does not compel us to agree with him. At the opening of the last Act he does, indeed, present Theseus as a sceptic. When Hippolyta remarks upon the strangeness of the lovers' accounts of their experience, he answers (Act V, Sc. 1, 2-6):

> More strange than true: I never may believe
> These antique fables, nor these fairy toys.
> Lovers and madmen have such seething brains,
> Such shaping fantasies, that apprehend
> More than cool reason ever comprehends.

But this practical, common-sense view is not accepted by Hippolyta; and she frowns on Theseus' scepticism (23-27).

> But all the story of the night told over,
> And all their minds transfigured so together,
> More witnesseth than fancy's images,
> And grows to something of great constancy;
> But, howsoever, strange and admirable.

Shakespeare's first dramatic use of the Supernatural is happy, gay, and sprightly. The only hint in this play of the darker, gloomier thought that was soon to supplant his youthful optimism is found in those cold, clammy lines about ghosts (Act III, Sc. 2, 380-387):

> . . . Yonder shines Aurora's harbinger;
> At whose approach, ghosts, wandering here and there,
> Troop home to churchyards: damned spirits all,
> That in crossways and floods have burial,
> Already to their wormy beds are gone;
> For fear lest day should look their shames upon,
> They wilfully themselves exile from light,
> And must for aye consort with black-brow'd night.

Here, it would seem, Shakespeare's thought wandered back to the malicious, inimical fairies of folk-lore, who were held by some to be the departed spirits of men and women, and for this reason were often confused with ghosts. We shall find a great deal in this strain in *Hamlet,* and still more in *Macbeth,* but it is not allowed to intrude into *Midsummer Night's Dream*. Oberon immediately dismisses this shadow on their careless joy with, "But we are spirits of another sort" (388).

While the Fairies intermingle with the humans in this first supernatural play, Shakespeare never allows us to forget the gulf between them – that they live in different worlds governed by different laws. This point is strongly emphasized in his later handling of the Supernatural, when his object has ceased to be light diversion and easy laughter, and has become the portrayal of tragedy in its most awe-inspiring and terrifying mood.

Although Shakespeare handles the Supernatural in *Midsummer Night's Dream* in such a jocular and irresponsible spirit, yet the comedy had a more profound influence on well-established superstition than any other play ever written. The Poet's original conception of fairies as tiny, benevolent, aery beings influenced all subsequent literature on the subject and finally dispelled the old ideas of malicious, evil, awful creatures who had to be obeyed and propitiated. The picture conjured up in our minds to-day by the word "fairy" is as different as could be to the repulsive fairy of the Elizabethans; and the change can be traced to Shakespeare and *Midsummer Night's Dream.*" [1]

1. See *The Elizabethan Fairies* (Latham).

By Cumberland Clark

Selected Criticisms

Wild and fantastical as this play is, all the parts in their various modes are well written, and give the kind of pleasure which the author designed. Fairies in his time were much in fashion; common tradition had made them familiar, and Spenser's poem had made them great.

Samuel Johnson

It is astonishing that Shakespeare should be considered, not only by foreigners, but by many of our own critics, as a gloomy and heavy writer, who painted nothing but "gorgons and hydras, and chimeras dire." His subtlety exceeds that of all other dramatic writers, insomuch that a celebrated person of the present day said that he regarded him rather as a metaphysician than a poet. His delicacy and sportive gaiety are infinite. In the *Midsummer Night's Dream* alone, we should imagine, there is more sweetness and beauty of description than in the whole range of French poetry put together. What we mean is this, that we will produce out of that single play ten passages, to which we do not think any ten passages in the works of the French poets can be opposed, displaying equal fancy and imagery.

William Hazlitt

Of all his works, the *Midsummer Night's Dream* leaves the strongest impression on my mind, that this miserable world must have, for once at least, contained a happy man. This play is so purely delicious, so little inter-mixed with the painful passions from which poetry distils her sterner sweets, so fragrant with hilarity, so bland and yet so bold, that I cannot imagine Shakespeare's mind to have been in any other frame than that of healthful ecstacy when the sparks of inspiration thrilled through his brain in composing it.

Thomas Campbell

Bottom the weaver is the representative of the whole human race. His confidence in his own power is equally profound, whether he exclaims, "Let me play the lion too"; or whether he sings alone, "that they shall hear I am not afraid"; or whether, conscious that he is surrounded with spirits, he cries out, with his voice of authority, "Where's Peasblossom?" In every situation Bottom is the same, – the same personification of that self-love which the simple cannot conceal, and the wise can with difficulty suppress.

Charles Knight

Here each kind of excellence is equal throughout; there are here no purple patches on a gown of serge, but one seamless and imperial robe of a single dye. Of the lyric or the prosaic part, the counterchange of loves and laughters, of fancy fine as air and imagination high as heaven, what need can there be for any one to shame himself by the helpless attempt to say some word not utterly unworthy? Let it suffice us to accept this poem as the landmark of our first stage, and pause to look back from it on what lies behind us of partial or of perfect work.

Algernon Charles Swinburne

In no other of his works has Shakespeare more brilliantly shown that complete dominance of theme which is manifested in the perfect preservation of proportion. The strands of action are braided with astonishing grace. The fourfold story is never allowed to lapse into dullness or obscurity. There is caprice, but no distortion. The supernatural machinery is never wrested toward the production of startling or monstrous effects, but it deftly impels each mortal personage in the natural line of human development. The dream-spirit is maintained throughout, and perhaps it is for this reason, – that the poet was living and thinking and writing in the free, untrammelled world of his own spacious and airy imagination, and not in any definite sphere of this earth, – that *A Midsummer Night's Dream* is so radically superior to the other comedies written by him at about this period.

William Winter

Enthralled by Shakespeare's art, and submissive to it, we accept without question every stroke of time's thievish progress, be it fast or slow; and, at the close, acknowledge that the promise of the opening lines has been redeemed. But if, in spite of all our best endeavors, our feeble wits refuse to follow him, Shakespeare smiles gently and benignantly as the curtain falls, and begging us to take no offence at shadows, bids us think it all as no more yielding than a dream.

Horace Howard Furness

Against the background of the whole play, which is only so much gossamer and moonlight, the honest weaver appears anything but romantic, a piece of humorous, bewildered flesh, gross, earthy. But if we view him first among his own associates, we shall see that he is the only one of them who was fit to be 'translated.' . . . He shows up as the romantic, the poetical, the imaginative man, who naturally takes command. We admit that he is conceited, but he is, in some measure, an artist, and artists are notoriously conceited.

J. B. Priestley

In *A Midsummer Night's Dream* all the best of Shakespeare's earlier poetry is woven into so comprehensive and exquisite a design that it is hard not to feel that this play alone is worth all the other romances. . . . In this play fairyland interpenetrates the world of human action. . . . The total result resembles those dreams, which yet, on waking, we find ourselves strangely regretting, loath to part from that magic even when it leaves nothing to the memory but incidents which should be painful.

G. Wilson Knight

The Midsummer Night's Dream, with all its appearance of fairy, with its apparent revelry in the stuff of which dreams are made, with its alluring unreality, and its evident riot of fantasy, is yet the first play in which Shakespeare reveals his promise as the world's comic dramatist, the first exhibition of his power to use comedy for its proper function, to show real man encountering the real problem of the world in which he was really living – in other words, for Shakespeare's day, the first play in which he showed contemporary man buffetted by the power felt than to the primary factor of his existence, his response to the quality and the might of love.

H. B. Charlton

No comedy of situation, not farce itself can provide a stranger encounter than that between Bottom and Titania; but it belongs to the purest comedy of character, and Bottom is as much the life of this scene as he is of the Interlude to follow. 'There is a sort of savage nobility about his firm reliance on his own bad taste,' says Professor Housman, speaking of the great Bentley's revision of *Paradise Lost;* and there is a similar robust independence in all Bottom's thoughts and actions that is not to be extinguished even by the ass's head. . . .

Peter Alexander

The world of this play is both veritable and large. It is not the tiny toy-shop that most such spectacles present, with quaint little people scampering on dry little errands, and with small music squeaking somewhere a childish accompaniment. There is room here for mortals no less than for fairies; both classes are at home, both groups move freely in a wide world where indeed they seem sometimes to have exchanged functions with one another. . . .

110

Had Shakespeare written nothing else than this he still might be the best of English poets.

Mark Van Doren

A Midsummer Night's Dream is the best of Shakespeare's early comedies. It has courtly interest, popular appeal, and a marvelous ingenuity in plot construction; there is no better managed multiple plot in the range of Elizabethan drama. This is the more remarkable because of the blending of varied elements and the creation of a dreamlike atmosphere. The plot of the wedding of Theseus and Hippolyta, the statesmanlike Theseus derived from Plutarch, forms, so to speak, the framework or border of the tapestry. The plot of the lovers, Demetrius and Helena, Lysander and Hermia, forms the central theme and is treated with such lightness of touch, such conventionality of style, such suggestion of youthfulness, that, in spite of its threatened griefs, it is not taken too seriously. The famous drama prepared by Bottom and his associates – "A tedious brief scene of young Pyramus and his love Thisbe; very tragical mirth" – is designed for the wedding of the royal personages. The fairy plot of Oberon and Titania ties the others together and serves to unify them. The king and queen of the fairies have come to Athens to attend the wedding; fairies are much interested in marriages and births. Oberon is jealous of Titania and Theseus, and rightly so; for Titania, who as a fairy has no social morals, has before this time assisted Theseus in some of his not too creditable love affairs. Titania pretends also to be jealous of Oberon and Hippolyta. Fairies get their recruits by the adoption of stray babies; therefore these jealousies are not marital but are jealousies of favor. When the disagreements of Oberon and Titania have been adjusted, they bless the marriage bed of Theseus and Hippolyta, and also of the lovers, whose difficulties they have likewise smoothed out. The weather accordingly improves.

The style of *A Midsummer Night's Dream* serves like color to illuminate and separate the plots. Theseus and Hippolyta, as royalty, speak in blank verse; the lovers speak usually in rhymed couplets, which formalize their troubles; the fairies appropriately employ a lyrical measure, trochaic tetrameter, except of course Oberon when he speaks as a king; the rustic actors speak in prose, the only appropriate medium and long conventionally employed for scenes of clownage; even the play of Pyramus and Thisbe has a meter of its own, a ballad measure as absurd as the play itself.

A Midsummer Night's Dream is thus a culmination of Shakespeare's early achievements in comedy. The play is a masterpiece in the weaving together into one story of a series of apparently unrelated plots, a method for which Shakespeare has always been famous. By his practice he refuted the classicists in drama in the matter of the unities, although the critical world down to the times of Dr. Samuel Johnson refused to see that he had done so. Dr. Johnson's enlightened common sense made him see that Shakespeare himself is the arbiter, since he never fails to attain his purpose: "as he commands us, we laugh or mourn, or sit silent with quiet expectation, in tranquility without indifference." As to variety in the picture of life, Johnson

111

says truly enough, "That the mingled drama may convey all the instruction of tragedy or comedy cannot be denied, because it includes both in its alternations of exhibition, and approaches nearer than either to the appearance of life, by showing how great machinations and slender designs may promote or obviate one another, and the high and low cooperate in the general system by unavoidable concatenation." That Shakespeare "approximates the remote and familiarizes the wonderful" enables him to show human nature "as it acts in real exigencies." With one strong puff from his manly chest Dr. Johnson blew away the fog of criticism surrounding Shakespeare's violations of the unities of time and place; for, said he, "The truth is, that the spectators are always in their senses, and know, from the first act to the last, that the stage is only a stage, and that the players are only players. Imitations produce pain or pleasure," he says, "not because they are mistaken for realities, but because they bring realities to the mind." Shakespeare himself was not ignorant of this principle if we may judge by the words which pass between Theseus and Hippolyta as they witness (Act V, Sc. 1, 212-16) the "Tedious brief scene of young Pyramus and his love Thisbe; very tragical mirth." She says

> This is the silliest stuff that ever I heard,

to which Theseus replies,

> The best of this kind are but shadows; and the worst are no worse, if imagination amend them.

She rejoins truly,

> It must be your imagination then, and not theirs.

There is a unity derivable from multiplicity, an ancient and natural form of art seen to this day in early tapestries and in oriental decorative art. . . .

Hardin Craig

Review Questions and Answers

Question 1.

Discuss the three worlds of the play. Be specific in your examples.

Answer

The four lovers inhabit one of the worlds of the play. Their situation is that of a stock thwarted romance, with the father demanding his daughter marry a man she doesn't love. The situation also includes a lovelorn maiden who has been abandoned by this same man. Although this situation contains the ingredients of tragedy, we see that the treatment is decidedly in a lighter, comic vein. Rather than a display of great passion and emotional strife, the speeches made are so stylized and formal that what we observe are the typical young lovers in the typical thwarted romance. We are meant to respond this way and are kept thus from feeling the deeper, stronger, more tragic emotions that are potentially present. A very formal verse form, stitchomythia, is employed in two places by the lovers. When the confusion is at its height in the woods, they do break out of their customary wooden mode and exhibit some true feeling. This is more true of the girls than of their boy friends, who persist in a rather shallow, trifling vein.

Another world in this play is occupied by the Athenian workmen. These characters are very, very different from the above. In contrast to the formal poetry that the lovers speak, these amiable simple men speak the prose of comic realism. Their situation is also markedly contrasted. The lovers become deluded and misled by illusion in the form of Puck's mischief with the love juice. The workmen undertake to deal with illusion in the form of a play they produce for Theseus' wedding. We are shown their rehearsal, which displays the great pains they take to explain away every illusion. To these men, reality and illusion are two entirely separate entities, and they insist upon stating which is which at every point where the slightest confusion might arise. They take absolutely no chances on this question. The manner in which their production goes forward is a classic expression of the position they represent on the reality-illusion question – a question at the heart of this play. When Bottom and his fellows deal with the moon, even that evanescent, inconstant body is brought down to earth and made to conform to their no-nonsense realism. Better have one of their own company represent moon than leave the matter up to that fleeting, shifting natural phenomenon. Of course, with the transformation of Bottom himself, this world partakes of the play's general confusion of reality and illusion. But Bottom is able to resolve this into a genuine union.

We gain entrance to yet a third world in this play. The fairy kingdom, presided over by Oberon and Titania, is Shakespeare's own creation. His fairies differ from those of folk tradition with respect to size, nature and activity. They are small, benevolent, and associated with flowers. Oberon and Titania speak poetry of great beauty. Puck's poetry is remarkable for rough vigor and a rustic flavor all its own. Puck, or Robin Goodfellow, is Oberon's lieutenant. His character and the poetry he speaks expressing it contrast with the delicate, airy fairies and their lyric verses. When the lovers enter the fairy world, their wooden, uninteresting speeches contrast with the flexibility and grace of speech in this other world.

Question 2.

How are these disparate and separate worlds joined in the play?

Answer

Although the workmen and the lovers are very different indeed, connections are established between the two groups as soon as we meet the second. Later, the fairies have a great deal to do with both groups. Finally all three groups come together at the court of Duke Theseus, the lovers are married, the workmen perform, and the fairies bless the household when everyone is asleep.

When we first meet the workmen, connections between them and the lovers we have already met are established as follows: (1) The reason these men are preparing a play is to entertain at that same wedding of Theseus and Hippolyta discussed in Scene 1, at which Hermia must announce her decision; (2) The subject of the play they have chosen, while comically distant from their own world, is relevant to Hermia's plight; (3) Their plan to rehearse the next night in the Duke's wood brings them into the same geographical area as the lovers who also plan to meet there. When Oberon overhears Helena pleading for Demetrius' love, the King of Fairies decides to help and this begins his interference in the lovers' world. The fairy world and that of the lovers interweave extensively when Puck mistakes Lysander for Demetrius, with all the ensuing complications. The mischievous goblin involves the workmen in his world of moonlight and magic by placing an ass's head on Bottom. Thus transformed, this down-to-earth tradesman becomes the intimate companion of Titania, Queen of Fairyland. Thus the power of fairy magic affects all three worlds and this is a cohesive force in the play. It binds together the separate strands that were marked to terminate in Theseus' marriage. In short, what we have in *A Midsummer Night's Dream* is a plot structure in which the marriage of Theseus and Hippolyta is the framing event in the daylight world. It is the first thing we hear of and the last thing that happens, but the cloth that is woven within this frame is of Oberon's design. He and his assistant Puck move the shuttle of this loom madly between the straight uprights of Theseus' frame. The lovers are matched as warp and woof, and Bottom's experience runs as a strong diagonal thread knitting all sturdily.

Question 3.

Discuss how the theme of change and transformation is present in this play.

Answer

There are a multitude of references to the theme of change and transformation, climaxing in Bottom's transformation and the change in the lovers' and Queen's eyesight. Finally a play is performed and this too concerns the theme under consideration, for art transforms reality. We should notice that the quarrel between Oberon and Titania is over a "changeling." It is the King's desire to have this boy which is the moving force behind the plot. Not only the cause but the result of the quarrel concerns change: Titania explains that the seasons have become all turned around as a result of the disorders in their royal household. Cause, result, and now solution concern change, for the solution of the quarrel is possible because of a change in a "little western flower" (a pansy). Furthermore, the change in the flower occurred at the same time that the Virgin Queen did not change. The arrow from Cupid's bow that was meant to change her, changed the flower instead. Finally, the power of this changed flower is to change people's eyesight so that the first creature they look upon immediately after the juice of the flower is applied is transformed into their beloved. In general, the moon, which presides over the whole play, is constantly changing from one phase to another. Both love and art look to the moon as their sovereign star, for both concern illusion and change. Art transforms reality, and we have been told over and over that love has to do not with constancy, but with change.

Question 4.

Point out the leading motifs or images in this play and describe their occurrences.

Answer

The use of one's eyes in love is introduced right at the beginning of the play when Theseus tries to convince Hermia to obey her father. The disobedient daughter says she wishes her father saw with her eyes. The Duke replies that her eyes ought to be governed by his judgment. When Oberon steps into the picture with his love juice, we see that linking judgment to vision in matters of love is not as straightforward as Theseus thinks it is. When Helena speaks of how the blind, winged boy, Cupid, is the appropriate governor of love, she too brings up the question of using one's eyes in love. This motif comes to a climax when Oberon and Puck apply the magic juice to Titania, Lysander and Demetrius. The charm is specifically directed at the eyes and under its spell a person looks and loves instantly. Judgment, reason, will, are all of no account whatsoever.

When the addled males protest that judgment, reason and will form the basis of their love, comedy is the result. After awakening from their enchanted experiences, Bottom and the lovers speak of what has happened in terms of eyesight. Demetrius says it's like trying to distinguish a landscape at a very great distance; Hermia feels as though she's seeing double; Helena can't believe her eyes. Bottom speaks of having had a ''most rare vision,'' which is a term most closely related to eyes. However, he properly widens it to include all the senses and says his vision passes beyond the evidence of all the senses. Flowers enter into the scene of this play in profusion. The fairy world that Shakespeare has created in this play is characterized in part by its association with flowers. In the scene where we first meet the fairies, nine flowers are mentioned. They continue to be mentioned throughout, and of course the love-charm is effected by use of the juice of a flower. The Duke's famous speech about ''single blessedness'' uses a flower to dramatize the argument.

The moon is a real presence in this play. It is mentioned many, many times and its light bathes the action of the play. At the very beginning of the play it is used by the Duke and his intended bride to measure the time until their wedding. Then the lovers make plans to meet by moonlight and elope. The workmen also plan to meet by moonlight in order to rehearse their play in privacy. The moon is important to this latter group in the further respect that they must have it in their play. Down-to-earth as they are, they have one of their own company represent Moonshine rather than leave the matter up to that shifting, fleeting celestial body. In short, the moon is sovereign of the night and it is "night-rule" that wreaks havoc in the woods.

Question 5.

Discuss the character of Bottom the weaver.

Answer

Nick Bottom the weaver is one of Shakespeare's most memorable creations. When we first meet him, the play "Pyramus and Thisbe" is being cast. Bottom is ready to take on anything. He has complete confidence in his ability to sweep from one end of the emotional scale to the other. The energy and enthusiasm with which he participates in life are immediately evident. Some critics have objected to what they consider his domineering, brash, self-centered personality, but this is a gross misunderstanding. When he shares Titania's bower, his easy graciousness with his extraordinary new companions is a mark of his marvellous ability to adapt immediately to whatever life offers him. His energetic love of life, his näiveté and eager innocence obtain his entrance into this other-world so different from his own. And he enjoys it to the fullest. When Bottom awakens from his "dream," his own manner of reacting to it is the best approach to the experience. Wonder, awe, and a strong sense of the power beyond man's apprehension are communicated by his words there. He rightly declares the unfathomability of his "dream" and feels most profoundly its power. He knows that it should be called "Bottom's Dream" for these correct reasons. Starting from his position as a rock-bottom realist, Bottom can, with the same vigor and joy he brings to whatever he does, respond to this power and believe. The fantastically transformed Bottom, the least likely candidate for the position in the world before his transformation, becomes a participator in the fairy world in the incredible role of being Titania's beloved. But we see thus that it was possible after all. He conducts himself with such sobriety and yet such grace, with his own good sense and yet with such enjoyment that we see he is a weaver in this deeper sense too – Bottom the weaver is supremely capable of uniting these disparate worlds. His very person embodies the union of reality and illusion, carrying as he does Puck's trick on his real, sturdy shoulders. His love of life enables him to engage in it to the fullest. The fullness of his engagement unites experiences. In this play where love and art and dreams assert their power over life, Bottom embodies the union of reality and illusion wherein lie the secret springs and mysterious force of life itself.

Question 6.

Sketch the character of Theseus.

Answer

In Theseus, Shakespeare has presented the picture of an English squire in Athenian garb. His love of hunting, his enthusiasm for sport, his devotion to

116

his hounds were as characteristic of the wealthy Englishman in Shakespeare's time as they are today. Dr. Dowden speaks of Shakespeare's supreme admiration of the heroic men of action – Theseus, Henry V, and Hector – and observes of Theseus: "There is no figure in the early drama of Shakespeare so magnificent. His are the large hands that have helped to shape the world. His utterance is the right-toned speech of one who is master of events – who has never known a shrill or eager feeling. His nuptial day is at hand; and while the other lovers are agitated, bewildered, incensed, Theseus, who does not think of himself as a lover, but rather as a beneficent conqueror, remains in calm possession of his joy. Theseus, a grand ideal figure, is to be studied as Shakespeare's conception of the heroic man of action in his hour of enjoyment and leisure. With a splendid capacity for enjoyment, gracious to all, ennobled by the glory, implied rather than explicit, of great foregone achievement, he stands at centre of the poem, giving their true proportions to the fairy tribe upon the one hand, and upon the other to the 'human mortals.' " He keeps his imagination well in hand, and speaks of the lovers' dreams and visions as 'antique fables' and 'fairy toys,' and yet he knows well that life is barren without imagination, and can find enjoyment in the honest attempts of imperfect actors. With his thoughts he can 'piece out their imperfections,' for he knows that in this kind of performance the best 'are but shadows, and the worst are no worse if imagination amend them.''

Question 7.

Describe generally the nature and habits which are attributed by Shakespeare to Puck.

Answer

PUCK'S NATURE   Puck, the "merry wanderer of the night," stands in a class by himself. He can hardly be said to possess a character, any more than the flowers of the field or the dreams which he brings to mortals. He acts as Oberon's lieutenant, and performs his errands and does his bidding, sometimes well and sometimes ill, but when he does ill, he feels no remorse, nor even regret; in fact, he rejoices when his ill-doing works result in mischief among the mortals he loves to torment.

HIS LOVE OF MISCHIEF   and his natural disposition for tricks have secured for him the role of jester in the court of King Oberon, who treats him with something of the indulgence accorded to a spoiled child. He is recognized as a "lob of spirits" by Titania's fairy, who knows him as a "shrewd and knavish sprite called Robin Goodfellow," that loves to frighten village maidens, mislead night wanderers,

> "And bootless make the breathless housewife churn;
> And sometime make the drink to bear no barm.''

AND OTHER QUALITIES   He is represented with a broom and has a preference for what is comely and clean over what is ugly or foul, but he always acts without any reference to principles of right and wrong. He is skilful in all transformations,

> "And neigh, and bark, and grunt, and roar, and burn,
> Like horse, hound, hog, bear, fire, at every turn."

The "jangling" of mortals is to him a sport, and the embarrassment of lovers a "fond pageant," for those things please him best "that befall preposterously." He enjoys flattery, and will even work for "those that Hobgoblin call him and sweet Puck." The beautiful Hermia in distress strikes for an instant a chord of pity in him, and the sight of Helena "curst and sad" makes him forget his own games for a moment and think of those of the god Cupid. He assures us at the close of the play that he is "an honest Puck," but there is certainly nothing in his actions which of itself would lead us to adopt this view of him.

Question 8.

What do you suppose to have been Shakespeare's purpose in introducing the play in the last act?

Answer

A Midsummer Night's Dream is of the nature of a Masque produced probably for some special occasion. One of the ordinary features of a masque was an anti-masque, designed to illustrate or parody the main story. The interlude of Pyramus and Thisbe serves this purpose. Delicate imaginative poetical feeling is replaced by grossness and comedy. Fairies are replaced by rude tradesmen, blank verse by prose, alliteration and doggerel, and love is made ridiculous by the hero and heroine of the piece.

Or we may say simply that Shakespeare introduces the interlude in order to fulfil a promise made in the first scene of the play. It has often been remarked that the opening scene is of great importance in striking the keynote of a play. (Compare the opening scenes of *Macbeth* and *A Merchant of Venice.*) In the opening scene of this play Theseus shows some weariness and a desire to hasten the passage of time, "to ease the anguish of a torturing hour," as he says, by witnessing some show.

> "Go, Philostrate,
> Stir up th' Athenian youth to merriments;
> Awake the pert and nimble spirit of mirth."

Philostrate does as he is bidden and the Interlude is the result.

Or we may describe Shakespeare's purpose in another way. We know that he was a master of the technique of the dramatic art, that he used at different times every device known to playwright to maintain the interest of his audience: mistaken identities, disguises, misunderstandings, surprising adventures, the exhibition of the supernatural, practical jokes, buffoonery. In order to hold the attention of his public he often introduced a secondary plot or a new phase of the theme. This he does here. In the play, Shakespeare frequently alludes to the power of imagination. It is a play of fancy. Puck, in the Epilogue, describes the play as a dream and the characters in it as shadows. By introducing the unimaginative Athenian craftsmen Shakespeare at the same time uses powerfully the dramatic device of contrast and gives Theseus an opportunity of teaching the necessity of imagination, not only in the presentation of a play, but also in an audience.

However, when all is said and done in explanation of Shakespeare's purpose, we cannot get away from the simple fact that he was a popular dramatist, neither academic nor classical, and that it may well have been the chief purpose of this comic interlude, coming after so much exquisite poetry, to serve as comic relief and to make the audience laugh.

Question 9.

What part does Titania take in the play? Introduce quotations in your answer.

Answer

The play is one in which the theme of love is lightly treated. The love of the mortals does not represent an abiding or profound sentiment, but is represented as being rather the effect of some visual enchantment, which it is in the power of the king of the faries to inspire. Such love, indeed, is seen undisguised and in its simplest form in Titania. She loves everything that is beautiful, but with no deep feeling. She delights in the pretty swimming gait of her mortal friend and in the lovely boy to whom her friend gave birth; she is attracted by flowers and dewdrops, birds and painted butterflies, and seeks to season life only with festivities and pleasures. There was jealousy between herself and Oberon, but, as Gervinus has remarked, "her resentment consists in separation, her reconciliation in a dance; there is no trace of a reflection, no indication of feeling. . . . when she awakens from her vision there is no reflection: 'Methought I was enamoured of an ass'; she says: 'O how mine eyes do loathe his visage now!' She is only affected by the idea of the actual and the visible." Such being her nature, Shakespeare, in depicting her infatuated with Bottom, wearing the features of a hairy ass, has painted a picture at the same time pathetic and irresistibly comic. She fondles him;

"Crowns him with flowers, and makes him all her joy,"

just as she had formerly petted her sweet changeling boy. Herein the poet has shown us something of the comedy of love, as, elsewhere, he has frequently depicted its tragedy. We may feel pity for her "dotage," as Oberon did when he met her.

"Seeking sweet favours for this hateful fool,"
but our pity will only be a transient feeling, as fleeting

119

"As that same dew, which sometime on the buds
Was wont to swell like round and orient pearls,"

and which

"Stood now within the pretty flowerets' eyes,
Like tears that did their own disgrace bewail,"

for we know that her infatuation cannot be lasting, and that it will leave no deeper trace upon her nature than "the fierce vexation of a dream."

Question 10.

Illustrate from the play Shakespeare's use of nature.

Answer

Shakespeare's observation of nature was that of a poet and an artist rather than that of a naturalist. It is true his accuracy of knowledge was in itself sufficiently wonderful in an age when little attention was paid to botany or to natural history; but what impresses us most in his treatment of nature is the marvellous wealth of knowledge of things great and small, which is to be found in lavish profusion in all his plays. This is evident not only, nor even principally, in his close observation of animals and habits, or in his intimate acquaintance with all varieties of flowers and their characteristics, but above all in his imagery, and in his descriptive expressions. The poet's knowledge of country life may be said to permeate the whole play of *A Midsummer Night's Dream*. It is such as could only have been acquired by one born and bred in the country, and possessing a sympathetic feeling for, and love of, everything pertaining to it. Not only is it exhibited in descriptive passages, but images faithfully copied from nature and accurately represented in words are blended with personal descriptions and in the most dramatic passages. Limits of space admit of a few illustrations only; the student will be able to swell out the number almost indefinitely. For convenience sake they are classified as follows:

IMAGERY   Notice how the poet, by metaphors and figures, apparently without any art or effort, condenses into single lines whole stores of past and possible experiences.

(a) "But earthlier happy is the rose distill'd" etc.

(Act I, Sc. 1, 76)

(b)   "Your tongue's sweet air
More tuneable than lark to shepherd's ear
When wheat is green, when hawthorn buds appear."

(Act I, Sc. 1, 183)

(c) "Two lovely berries moulded on one stem."

(Act III, Sc. 2, 211)

(d) "You minimus of hindering knot-grass made."

(Act III, Sc. 2, 331)

Observe again, the delicacy of artistic feeling and the gorgeous colouring in the following:

(e) (Phoebe) "decking with liquid pearl the bladed grass."

(Act I, Sc. 1, 211)

(f) "Even till the eastern gate, all fiery-red,
Opening on Neptune with fair blessed beams,
Turns into yellow gold his salt-green streams."

(Act III, Sc. 2, 393)

What a picture is called up by Oberon's picture of Titania's bower: "I know a bank where the wild thyme blows," etc.

DESCRIPTIVE EXPRESSIONS   Note, among others, the following: "Faint primrose beds," "the cowslips tall," "the nodding violet," "weaving spiders," "long'legg'd spinners," "plain-song cuckoo," "russet-pated choughs," "red-hipped humble bee on the top of a thistle."

KNOWLEDGE OF ANIMALS   Note the accuracy and precision with which the tones of a pack of hounds are described in: "Match'd in mouth like bells, each under each." In this passage much knowledge and observation are conveyed in few words.

Question 11.

Show how Shakespeare varies his verse according to the character of the speaker or the nature of the theme.

Answer

The fairies usually speak in rhymed verse, as should delicate and poetic beings, but they use blank verse when they quarrel (Act II, Sc. 1, 60, etc.). In Act III, Sc. 1, 155-160 we have a series of six rhyming lines repeating a single sound, perhaps to mark the very strong contrast between the poetry of Titania and the grossness of Bottom. *A Midsummer Night's Dream* being one of Shakespeare's earlier plays, the changes of metre, which are designed by the poet to produce an emotional effect, are not so numerous as in some later plays. The following points, however, will be found worthy of consideration. Act I, Sc. 1, is in blank verse as far as line 171. Lines 171-8 contain the expression of a single thought, and are in rhyme. Previous to 171, the conversation had been more or less business-like, but the entrance of Helena gives rise to a more emotional theme, which is expressed in rhyme. Soliloquies, the quiet outpourings of meditative thought, are usually in rhymed verse, as at the end of Act I, Sc. 1 and Act II, Sc. 2. In the latter case, Hermia's excitement is denoted by the irregularity of the accent. Contrast with these passages the utterance of Theseus at the beginning of Act V. Here the comparative frequency with which the feminine ending occurs serves to distinguish the wise philosophy of Theseus from the more romantic and poetical character of the language of the other people, and at the same time reproduces, to some extent, the easy tone of ordinary life. Notice, again, the change from rhyme to blank verse in Act III, Sc. 2, 194, marking the excitement of the speakers, still further denoted by the number of feminine endings, increasing with the growing passion of the speakers.

Bibiliography

Adams, Joseph Quincy. *A Life of William Shakespeare*. New York: Houghton-Mifflin Co., 1923.

Alexander, Peter. *Shakespeare*. London: Oxford University Press, 1964.

Barber, C. L. *Shakespeare's Festive Comedy*. Princeton: Princeton University Press, 1959.

Berry, Ralph. *Shakespeare's Comedies: Explorations in Form*. Princeton: Princeton University Press, 1972.

Bethell, S. L. *Shakespeare and the Popular Drama Tradition*. London: King and Staples, 1944.

Briggs, Katherine M. *The Anatomy of Puck*. London: Routledge and Paul, 1959.

Brown, John Russell. *Shakespeare and his Comedies*. London: Methuen and Co., 1957.

Chambers, E. K., ed. *A Midsummer Night's Dream* (The Arden Shakespeare). Revised by Edith Rickert. Boston: D. C. Heath & Co., 1916.

Clemen, W. *The Development of Shakespeare's Imagery*. London: Methuen and Co., 1951.

Craig, Hardin. *An Interpretation of Shakespeare*. New York: Dryden Press, 1948.

_____, ed. *A Midsummer Night's Dream in Shakespeare*, revised ed. New York: Scott, Foresman and Co., 1958.

De La Mare, Walter. *"Introduction,"* in *A Midsummer Night's Dream*. C. Aldred, ed. London: The Macmillan Company, 1935.

Doran, Madeleine, ed. *A Midsummer Night's Dream* (The Pelican Shakespeare). Baltimore: Penguin Books, 1959.

Ellis-Fermor, Una M. *Shakespeare the Dramatist*. London: Geoffrey Cumberlege, 1948.

Furness, Horace Howard, ed. *A Midsummer Night's Dream*. Philadelphia: Lippincott, 1895.

Gibson, H. N. *The Shakespeare Claimants*. New York: Barnes & Noble, Inc. 1962.

Goddard, Harold C. *The Meaning of Shakespeare*. Chicago: University of Chicago Press, 1951.

Herbert, T. Walter. *Oberon's Mazed World*, Baton Rouge: Louisiana State University Press, 1977.

Muir, Kenneth. "Pyramus and Thisbe: A Study in Method," in *Shakespeare Quarterly V*. New York: Shakespeare Association of America, 1954.

Noble, Richmond. *Shakespeare's Use of Song*. London: Oxford University Press, 1925.

Palmer, John. *Comic Characters of Shakespeare*. London: The Macmillan Company, 1946.

Parrott, Thomas Marc. *Shakespeare Comedy*. New York: Oxford University Press, 1949.

Priestley, J. B. *The English Comic Characters*. London: The Bodley Head, 1925; reprinted 1963.

Purdom, C. B. *What Happens in Shakespeare*. London: John Baker, 1963.

Sidgwick, Frank. *The Sources and Analogues of "A Midsummer Night's Dream."* London: Chatto and Windus, 1908.

Sitwell, Edith. *A Notebook on William Shakespeare*. London: Oxford University Press, 1928.

Watkins, Ronald. *Moonlight At the Globe*. London: Michael Joseph, 1946.

Welsford, Enid. *The Court Masque*. Cambridge: University Press, 1927.

Wilson, J. Dover. *The Essential Shakespeare*. New York: Cambridge University Press, 1932.

_____ *Shakespeare's Happy Comedies*. London: Oxford University Press, 1962.

NOTES